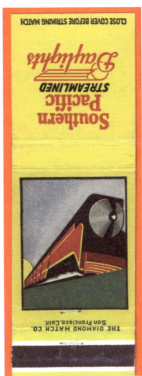

El Camino Real *by Minnie M. Tingle*

Full many leagues, in sinuous curves it lies
    'Cross sands where buried rest old memories sweet,
    Of half-forgotten days when sandaled feet
Trod there on mission brave. The warm light dies
Amid the tangled weeds from whence arise
    Mute voices vocal with a tale replete
    With life's primordial forces ere effete
And more ignoble forms stalked in disguise.

    But whether by the strand where sea-gulls call;
        Or deep in sunless recess of the wood;
            (And where, perchance, some prayer-rapt padre stood);
        On slopes where vagrant poppies spill their gold;
        Or yet within the desert's hungry hold,
            The trail of brown robe lies over all.

El Camino Real — Highway 101

Tom Zimmerman, *with* Roger L. Titus

& The Route of the *Daylight*

Los Angeles Railroad Heritage Foundation

El Camino Real — Highway 101 & the Route of the Daylight
© 2013 Los Angeles Railroad Heritage Foundation
www.larhf.org   email: info@larhf.org

Designed by Schoenehauser

Dust jacket illustration by Beverly Lazor

All rights reserved. No part of this book may be reproduced or transmitted in any form or by any means, electronic or mechanical, including photocopying, recording, or by an information storage and retrieval system, without express written permission from the publisher.

Names and trademarks of products are the property of their registered owners.

Library of Congress Cataloging-in-Publication Data

El Camino Real — Highway 101 & the Route of the Daylight by Tom Zimmerman with Roger L. Titus; editor in chief: Josef K. Lesser; designer: Kurt Hauser.

Summary: Using photographs, post cards, and ephemera, El Camino Real — Highway 101 & the Route of the *Daylight* tells the story of transportation on the coastal route in nineteenth and twentieth-century California. Stagecoaches, railroads, and automobiles all played a role in connecting coastal California's mission towns, military bases, agricultural centers and petroleum fields with the major cities of Los Angeles, San Jose and San Francisco.

Includes bibliographical references, index, and credits.

ISBN 978-0-11620-4
1. Transportation-California-History-nineteenth century. 2.Transportation-California-History-twentieth century. 3.Railroads-California-History-nineteenth century.
4. Railroads-California-History-twentieth century. 5. California Missions.
6. California Agriculture. 7. California Petroleum production. 8. California-History-Pictorial works. 9. California-Military history.

Poem on page one: Minnie May Orewyler Tingle (1874-1926) was a Los Angeles based artist and poet. She painted the complete ladder of missions in 1924 and exhibited them at the Los Angeles Exposition Park's Museum of History, Science and Art in 1925. On her death the following year, her husband, T. R. Tingle, donated the entire series to the museum and printed a book of her mission paintings and poems called, *California Missions and Mission Sites Along the Kings Highway* in 1924.

Page 2: Mission San Miguel courtyard with a statue of Father Junipero Serra facing El Camino Real. Highway 101 and the *Daylight* railroad tracks are in the background.

Page 3: Restored *Daylight* locomotive No. 4449 crossing the Gaviota trestle in Santa Barbara County.

This page: Restored *Daylight* locomotive No. 4449 pulling out of the Los Angeles Union Station, May 5, 1989

Contents

9	Foreword
11	Acknowledgments
13	Introduction
19	Post Cards Say it Better
21	Producer of the Finest Post Cards

ONE El Camino Real — Ladder of the Missions
25

TWO Highway 101 — In the Beginning
51

THREE The Route of the *Daylight*
85

FOUR Three Towns — Bradley, San Miguel, and Buellton
113

FIVE Two Towns — San Jose and San Luis Obispo
125

SIX One Town — Santa Barbara
143

NINE The Route of the Military
177

SEVEN Green Gold — A Bountiful Land
153

TEN A Place to Stop — Along the Way
187

EIGHT Black Gold — Derricks & Rockers
169

201   Epilogue
204   Bibliography
205   Index
208   Illustration Credits

Foreword

"Just Yesterday"

It was 1944; my mom took Larry (my younger brother) and me to San Gabriel to see "The Mission Play." Soon afterward in our family car, my parents, my brothers Larry and Bob, and I traveled to San Diego to visit relatives. In those days Highway 101 was always an adventure. The drive took at least six hours, depending on the stops we'd make. The first stop was always Philippe's French Dip sandwiches on Aliso Street immediately across from the Los Angeles Union Passenger Terminal (LAUPT). Our noon picnic was the best part of the day, usually spent at Knott's Berry Farm in Buena Park. It seems that no matter what time we left Los Angeles and after checking into our hotel, we would arrive at my aunt and uncle's at 6:00 p.m., just in time for dinner. Aunt Helen was a terrific cook.

There were always two sightseeing highlights that we visited, the San Diego Zoo and the San Diego Mission. Having seen "The Mission Play," I knew there were twenty more missions somewhere in California, and I wanted to see them all. With World War II ended and gasoline rationing over, my parents decided to take us on a summer trip from Los Angeles to Vancouver, Canada, and back. That was my first of many, many rides north on Highway 101, El Camino Real.

We followed Highway 101 through Ventura, which at the time was Main Street and the location of the Buenaventura Mission. North of Ventura we toured the missions in Santa Barbara, San Luis Obispo, San Miguel, and the most northern mission San Rafael. A few years later I visited many more of the missions, and by 1956 I had visited all twenty-one.

It never occurred to me that the Southern Pacific railroad tracks, Highway 101, and many of the historic missions were only a short distance from each other. This was no coincidence, as we shall learn in this book.

One of the Los Angeles Railroad Heritage Foundation's (LARHF) primary missions is the publication of books. The other missions include its public outreach programs and archival preservation. The non-profit 501(c)(3) organization also operates the archival photo-rich website, www.larhf.org.

Advertising the *Mission Play*, photographed by the Southern California Edison Company on April 12, 1915. The Elden Hotel was built in 1894 and was located at 548 South Broadway in downtown Los Angeles. The photograph is from the Southern California Edison Collection in the Henry Huntington Library. San Marino, California

The Foundation's most recent book, *Route 66 – Railway*, tells of the close relationship between Route 66 and the Santa Fe Railway. The book's successful sale prompted LARHF to next publish this book about Highway 101 and the *Daylight*, but we could hardly write about those two icons without looking at how a third icon, the California Missions ties them altogether. Tom Zimmerman was a perfect choice to write this book with his in-depth knowledge of California, his photography career, and collection of California ephemera. Tom's book, *Paradise Promoted: The Selling of Los Angeles, 1870-1930* is a perfect complement to *El Camino Real – Highway 101 & the Route of the Daylight*.

A good friend and benefactor of the Foundation, Roger L. Titus, possesses a world-class vintage post card collection, and what better way to illustrate pre-photography sights than the use of colorful post cards? Not only did Roger make his post cards available for this book but he also shared his knowledge of the history and importance of post cards in the promotion of California in the late 1800s and early 1900s.

The search for rarely seen photographs to illustrate the book was like a treasure hunt! My wife, Jo Ann, and I traveled up and down Highway 101 more than once, visiting photo repositories and going to Sacramento to look at photographs from the California State Library and Caltrans. The deeper the search, the more nice surprises we uncovered. These archival gems continued to come to our attention until we had to call a stop and continue with the next phase of the book's production. With all the materials we gathered, there will have to be a companion volume.

It took over a year to formulate the contents for the book and another year to produce it. For me, seeing the "Mission Play" in 1944 left a lasting impression and perhaps inspired this book.

Today, the "Mission Play" is once again being produced, re-imagined, for audiences. It is a notable achievement that this play, first produced in 1912 to celebrate the romance of early California, is still entertaining and relevant 100 years later.

I am a native Californian and today, driving Highway 101 or riding the *Coast Starlight* is always an emotional trip for me, and with this book I celebrate the unique combination of California icons: the missions, El Camino Real, and the "most beautiful train in the world."

Josef K. Lesser, CEO – Los Angeles Railroad Heritage Foundation
February 2013

Acknowledgments

Visualizing Tom Zimmerman's excellent manuscript and working with Roger Titus and his treasure of vintage post cards were just the beginning. Our search became a treasure hunt to find archival photographs and ephemera for illustrating our book, *El Camino Real — Highway 101 & the Route of the Daylight.*

Both Tom and Roger are professional photographers who made available to LARHF their personal collections and took contemporary photographs for the book.

Of monumental value were the photos and ephemera loaned to LARHF by: Mark Borja, Leif Casagrande, Greg Ellison, Steve George, Paul Jansson, Mike Jarel, Paul C. Koehler, Phill Laursen, Bob Lowman, Bruce Petty, Brad Rocca, and Lora Schraft. A special thanks to Christopher Silva, Order of Capuchin Friars Minor, who posed with the El Camino Real bell at Mission Santa Ynez.

Many of the institutional sources we visited were wonderfully helpful. Their representatives clearly understood our objective to illustrate the book with fresh and unusual photographs.

We began our research in the greater Los Angeles area, and the following sources are to be especially thanked: Automobile Club of Southern California (Matthew Roth and Morgan P. Yates); Bison Archives (Marc Wanamaker); Huntington Library (Alan Jutzi); Los Angeles Public Library (Christina Rice); Pasadena Museum of History (Jeannette O'Malley and Anuja Navare); and Seaver Center for Western History Research (John M. Cahoon).

Beyond southern California we received significant assistance from: Buellton Historical Society (Curt Cragg); California Department of Transportation Library and History Center (Janet Coles and Shubhangi Kelekaro); California Room, San Jose Public Library; California State Archives; Crocker Art Museum (Andrew Blicharz); Gilroy Museum (Tom Howard and Phill Laursen); History Center of San Luis Obispo County (Erin Newman and Allan Ochs); National Park Service, Fort Hunter Liggett Special Resources Study; Paso Robles Historical Society; Sourisseau Academy for State & Local History, San Jose State University (Stephanie Waslohn and Leilani Marshall); Museum of Ventura County (Charles N. Johnson); Naval Base Ventura County (NBVC) Port Hueneme/Point Mugu; and Vandenberg Air Force Base, 30th Space Wing, Community Relations (Larry Hill).

A major thank you goes to the team that helped finalize and prepare the manuscript for Kurt Hauser's creative design. Abraham Hoffman proofread the manuscript; Larry Mullaly with his expertise of the Southern Pacific Railroad critiqued, Chapter 3; Wendell Mortimer, president of LARHF, proofread the manuscript in its final stage; Jeremy Rosenberg copy-edited the Forward; Roger Carp, senior editor at *Classic Toy Trains* magazine, did the final copyediting; and Jo Ann Lesser made the final compilation of the manuscript with its index and photo credit list. The book's attractive dust jacket is an original painting by Beverly Lazor.

The financing for this book's publication was entirely underwritten by LARHF's members and benefactors: Francis and Margaret Butler, Robert and Dennis De Pietro, Ron and Nadya Gustafson, Deke Keasbey, Ellie and Mark Lainer, Michael and Aliza Lesser, Captain Walter and Margrette Lester, USN Ret., Wendell and Ceil Mortimer, Edgar A. Romo, Jr., James G. and Virginia L. Roodhouse, Dr. Stephen J. Skahen, and J. Ross and Valerie J. Urquhart

The next book is already in its planning stages. Announcements regarding LARHF's future publications can be found on its website: larhf.org.

Josef K. Lesser, Editor in chief

Introduction

The Coast Route known as Highway 101 between San Diego and San Francisco is the great historic route in California. It follows the route of the first road in California, El Camino Real, which connected the first towns and outposts of California. Translated as "the King's Highway," it was carved out of the state by the original Spanish explorers, padres, soldiers, and merchants.

The route of the Southern Pacific Railroad's *Daylight* train was completed in 1901, after a lengthy thirty-six year struggle building tunnels, trestles, extensive excavations, and huge loops. This coastal route practically parallels El Camino Real from Los Angeles to San Francisco. In the mid-1930s, at the height of the Great Depression, Southern Pacific President Angus McDonald spotlighted the route by inaugurating the streamlined red, orange, and black *Coast Daylight* passenger train, called "the most beautiful train in the world."

Highway 101 was one of the original United States highways in 1926 and became the third transportation route through the most historic part of California.

The King's Highway was the unpaved, unmarked path that snaked north out of Mexico to connect the missions, military presidios, and pueblos of Spanish California. It started with the overland expedition led by Gaspar de Portola in 1769 from Baja California to establish a military presence, or presidio, on the fabled bay of Monterey, which was first explored and named by the sea-going expedition led by Sebastian Vizcaino in 1602. A key member of Portola's group was Father Junipero Serra, who was president of the missions in California. The missions were to play a key role in the Spanish dominance of coastal California. They were meant to be both religious and civil entities that would bring Christianity to the Indians while organizing them to solidify Spain's control over Alta California. Serra realized all that, but he was dedicated to bringing Christianity to the people even though most Spanish perceived the Indians as lost in heathenism. He perceived the missions to be a "ladder" through California. What connected the rungs of that ladder was El Camino Real.

The Franciscan mission ladder was short-lived. The first mission at San Diego was founded in 1769. The nineteenth mission at Santa Ynez opened in 1804, with two smaller missions constructed in the San

Painting commissioned by the Southern Pacific Company entitled, "California for the Tourist" and introduced on an advertising brochure printed in 1930.

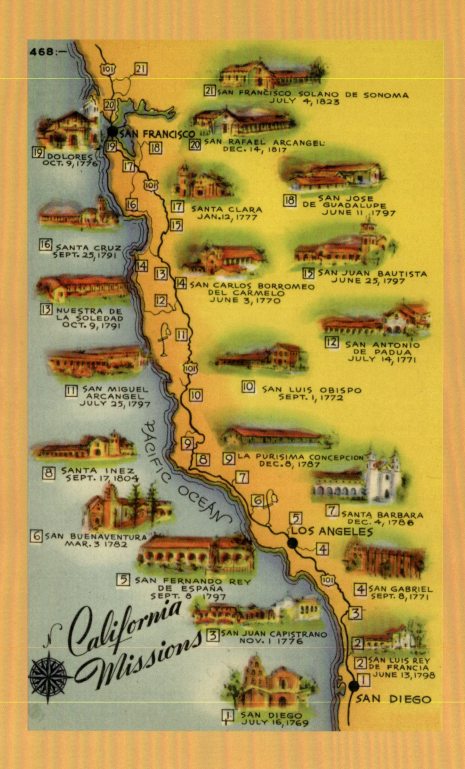

ALONG THE SHORE OF THE PACIFIC AT SUNSET

Francisco Bay area in 1817 and 1823. Following the successful outcome of Mexico's war for independence in 1821 and the subsequent secularization of the missions, the buildings began to decline rapidly, as most of the priests and virtually all the remaining Indians left and the land was sold by representatives of the Mexican government. The American conquest in 1847 and California's eventual statehood in 1850 sealed the fate of the Catholic structures and the adobe bricks that were the major structural component of the buildings gave way to earthquakes, weather, and neglect.

With the coming of the twentieth century, California had already been engaged in a promotional campaign to lure settlers out "west of the west" as President Theodore Roosevelt put it. As the campaign passed from the railroads to chambers of commerce, the creation of a romantic past became part of the promotion. Helen Hunt Jackson's novel *Ramona*, written in 1884 set the tone. It told the tragic story of the maiden Ramona and her Indian lover Alessandro killed by a Yankee who thought he had stole a horse. The entire novel is filled with melancholy for an Indian way of life disappearing in the face of the American onslaught. The Spanish past is seen as a hopelessly lost ideal. The promoters started calling this romantic myth, the "Days of the Dons." Mexicans were largely ignored in all this. The myth had to do with the noble Spanish

landowners, loyal soldiers, loving and hardworking Franciscan padres, and humble Indians eager to be saved. A key component to this was El Camino Real, which connected them all.

The Spanish chose the route well. When the Southern Pacific Railroad built its first lines into the Salinas Valley from San Francisco in the 1880s to haul agricultural products, the line largely followed the King's Highway. It continued to do so as the line was extended south to connect with Los Angeles. When local jurisdictions and the state of California began constructing paved roads to accommodate automobiles and trucks through the area, El Camino Real was again the template. Once the federal government decided to construct a national highway system in the 1920s to replace the haphazard group of named roads that started the national highway system, the far western north-south highway designated US 101 largely followed the Spanish footpath.

When United States Highway 101, or "the Coastal Route," was dedicated in 1922, it connected the original pueblos (San Jose and Los Angeles) with the original presidios (San Francisco, Monterey, Santa Barbara, and San Diego,) and all twenty-one of the missions that were rapidly coming to the fore in the nascent California tourist industry. The early twentieth century found most of the missions in disrepair or actual ruin. Charles Fletcher Lummis' Landmarks Club of Southern California had started raising money and awareness to rehabilitate the buildings in 1895.

The post-World War II boom in automobile tourism would find the missions largely saved and open for viewing. Highway 101 would serve as a fine modern road to take people to them. As early as 1921, Thomas Murphy was pointing out in his book about "motor rambles in California," that you could expect to take three days using the "inland route" to drive from San Diego to San Francisco while the "coast run" would take four.

Interstate 5 has taken over from Highway 99 as the faster inland route today, while 101 takes several hours longer. But while 101 proceeds leisurely past the original towns and cities of the state, up the comfortably narrow Salinas Valley while constantly flirting with the Pacific Ocean, Interstate 5 purposely skirts any and all towns in the broad, mundane, albeit massively fertile, Valley of the San Joaquin. For beauty, changing scenery, and the chance to visit small town California, there is no comparison between the two routes. As a bonus, every thirty to fifty miles the 101 gives you a chance to visit one of the key aspects of the state's history – the Alta California Mission System.

The story of Highway 101, the missions, and the route of the *Daylight* is the history of the state of California. From its earliest days as a path only wide enough to accommodate a horse or ox-drawn cart between the missions to its current multi-laned divided road that is an interstate highway for most of its length, 101 has always been the most significant roadway in the state. It has largely disappeared beneath Interstate 5 from Los Angeles south to San Diego, but the route north to San Francisco and beyond is as popular and utilized as ever. Today, Amtrak's *Coast Starlight* has replaced the Southern Pacific's *Daylight*. The Los Angeles and San Francisco-San Jose megalopolises have overwhelmed the small towns that were formerly only in their orbit. Santa Barbara remains a major tourist attraction, while Ventura pumps oil – on shore and off shore – and is home to strategic Air Force installations. Salinas and King City are major packing and shipping areas for the "Nation's Salad Bowl." Buellton is still home to the most famous pea soup in the United States and remains the gateway to the increasingly famous Santa Barbara County vineyards. Connecting with the intermittent California Highway 1 that runs right next to the Pacific Ocean through Malibu and Big Sur, Highway 101 takes you through the spectacularly varied landscape and history of coastal California. It is the sovereign of the California highways.

Why Write a Letter When Post Cards Say it Better!

Post cards are integral to the history of Highway 101. For over a half-century tourists along the coastal route could buy inexpensive colorful reminders of where they had been or wished to go. The buyer either saved the cards as souvenirs or sent them to friends and relations back home. This deluge of mail was a result of the Private Mailing Act of May 19, 1898, which allowed private firms in the United States to print cards. It was an economical way to stay in touch. From its inauguration until January 1, 1952 it cost only a penny to send greetings from the road.

The first regularly printed post cards were produced in Hungary in 1870 and soon spread to the rest of Europe. The first American souvenir cards were printed for the 1893 Columbian Exposition in Chicago. They required the full two cents postage that was charged at that time. The big change came with the Private Mailing Act of 1898. Prior to this the only post cards that could be mailed for a penny were governmentally printed cards.

After the passage of the Act post cards spread like wildfire as more people began traveling in the 20th century. Every hotel, motel, restaurant, town and roadside attraction printed a memory of itself. The first were printed in black and white, but soon the companies started hand coloring the images. Black and white "real photo" cards became common in the 1930s. The "photo chrome" cards that was common after World War II supplanted them. Color, digitally based, images continue to dominate the current post card market.

The cards continue to live up to publisher Curt Teich's 1910 observation, "Why write a letter when post cards say it better?" For just a couple of dollars any tourist can come home with dozens of colorful reminders of their trip while having quickly and easily stayed in touch with those near and dear. Anyone can have a small stack of evocative memories of the sites they saw or missed and the places they stayed.

Message side of vintage post cards

Producer of the Finest Post Cards

Above: Edward H. Mitchell comic post card No. 626, ca 1905

Opposite: Collage of Edward H. Mitchell post cards depicting scenes of San Francisco, ca 1910

Following pages: California Official Tourist Picture Map produced by the All-Year Club, 1936

Edward H. Mitchell published some of the finest early post cards. He was born in San Francisco on April 27, 1867, went to local schools, and worked for A.L. Bancroft and Company selling books and stationary supplies. As he moved up at Bancroft, he started to increase his income by selling souvenir items. In 1893, that developed into the Edward H. Mitchell Company, which printed and distributed post cards.

Mitchell was not a photographer or a dreamer. He was a practical businessman who created thousands of cards over the years that concentrated on West Coast scenes but included cards showing other points in the United States and around the world. He created specialty card series to commemorate the 1906 San Francisco earthquake and the 1915 Panama Pacific International Exposition and scenes of Hawaii and the Philippines. The cards were created using black-and-white photographs that were beautifully hand-colored and sometimes augmented to improve the looks of the moon, put a hat on someone, and whatever else Mitchell thought would improve the look of the card. The post card featuring the Tower of Jewels at the Panama-Pacific International Exposition included glitter that was glued on by Mitchell's daughters. Included in his inventory were all the scenic spots and significant buildings along the coast route, particularly the missions.

Mitchell also released cards through the Pacific Novelty Company and the Souvenir Publishing Company, but it was his own company that captured most of his energy and imagination. He was very proud of the fact that the Edward H. Mitchell Company was the first lithographing factory to give their workers the eight-hour day. Mitchell got out of the post card business in 1923. The three and one-half million cards that remained were sold in Los Angeles for $500. He was already president of the Edward H. Mitchell Oil Company and continued in that position until he retired in 1928.

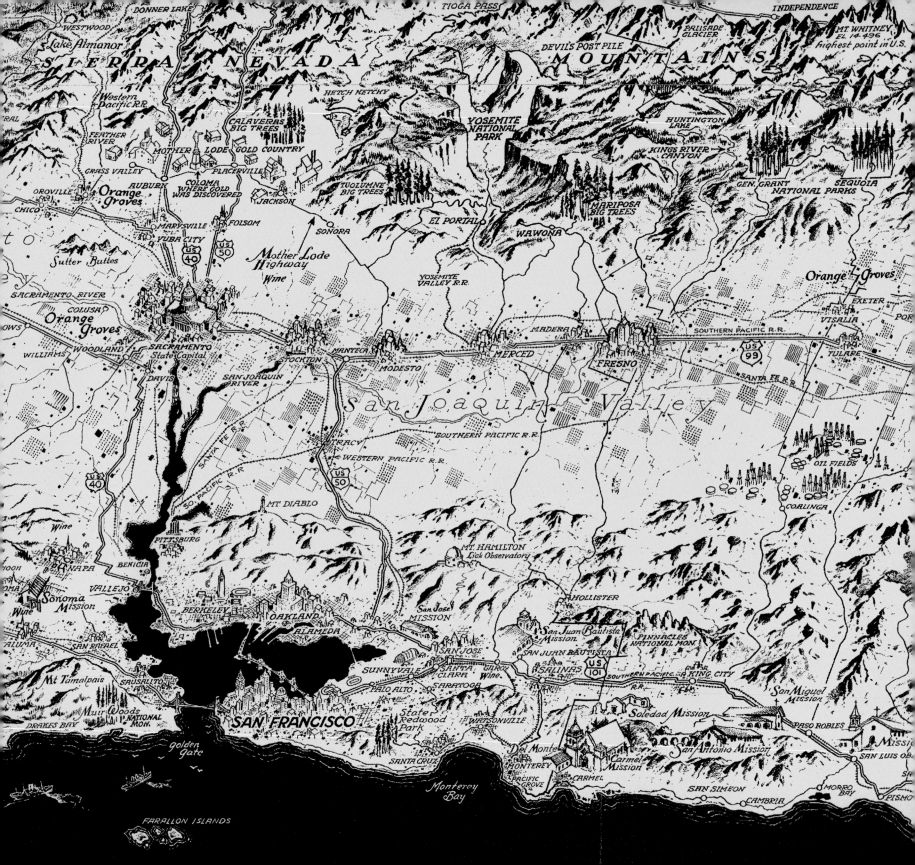

Chapter One

El Camino Real • The Ladder of the Missions

El Camino Real—the King's Highway or the Royal Road meandered north from San Diego to the far side of the Golden Gate and was the key land route through the Spanish colony. A party of soldiers and Franciscan padres led by Captain Gaspar de Portola first scouted it out in 1769. His party left Velicata, Baja California in May and established the first Alta California mission at San Diego in July. Leading the padres was the man who would become Father President and founder of the California mission chain, Junipero Serra. Father Serra stayed in San Diego to build the first mission and begin the conversion of the natives. Portola, along with Father Juan Crespi as chaplain and diarist accompanied by sixty-three soldiers and over one hundred mules, moved on to find a land route to the Bay of Monterey.

As it happened, they passed by, not seeing, Monterey Bay but found San Francisco Bay, which had been obscured by fog and missed by ocean going explorers. The party finally returned to San Diego in January 1770. In their coming and going, they established what would remain the general route of El Camino Real. Portola traveled the same route north again in April and this time found Monterey Bay. Father Serra opted to travel north by sea and arrived shortly after Portola had set up camp. The captain set about establishing the presidio at Monterey while Father Serra worked to create Mission San Carlos Borromeo de Carmelo, the second of the California missions.

Mission San Diego de Alcalá, 1957

Statue of Father Junipero Serra in Golden Gate Park, San Francisco, ca. 1915

Mural in Bank of America, Treasure Island Branch, 1939

Portola's expedition in 1769 was ordered due to the interest being shown by England and Russia in Alta California. The long-range idea was to establish coastal military bases at San Diego, Santa Barbara, Monterey, and San Francisco, all of which would be fed by the agricultural products of established towns ("pueblos") at San Jose, Los Angeles, and Branciforte (near present-day Santa Cruz). The natives of the state would be Christianized and Europeanized by Franciscan padres, who would establish what Father Serra called a "ladder" of missions through Alta California. The missions would also provide food for the presidios as well as establish a Spanish presence throughout the colony and work to convert the natives and make them productive, non-hostile members of a Spanish colonial society. The rungs on Serra's ladder would eventually consist of twenty-one missions stretching north from San Diego to Sonoma (north of San Francisco) that were essentially one day's horseback ride, or three day's walk, apart on El Camino Real.

For some sixty years, the Franciscans in the ladder of missions stretching along El Camino Real served both the Spanish king and the "King of Kings" as they worked to reconstruct the lives of the Indians in their care.

Most of the missions had seen success in attracting converts and achieving self-sufficiency. Mission Dolores in San Francisco was an exception, as it did not prosper in either its political or religious roles. Mission San Gabriel was incredibly successful, serving a population of 1,701 neophytes in 1817. It also had the largest winery and most productive agricultural fields of any of the missions. A year earlier, Mission San Buenaventura had a population of 1,328.

Santa Barbara and La Purisima Concepcion near Lompoc peaked in 1804 with populations of 1,792 and 1,520, respectively. Even isolated Mission Soledad in 1804 attracted 687 neophytes to its extremely productive agricultural fields. Mission San Luis Rey forty-one miles north of San Diego prospered a little later.

Mission San Miguel – "The Route of the Padres"

The Missions

San Diego de Alcalá, 10818 Mission Road, San Diego. Founded 1769

San Luis Rey de Francia, off Highway 76, Oceanside. Founded 1798

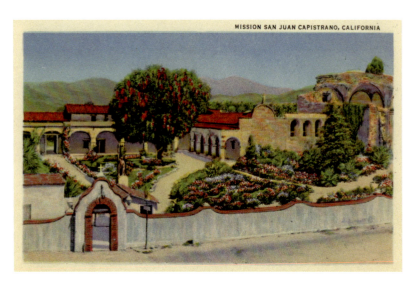

San Juan Capistrano, off I-5 at Ortega. Founded 1776

San Gabriel Arcángel, 428 South Mission Drive. Founded 1771

San Fernando Rey de España, 15151 San Fernando Mission Boulevard. Founded 1797

San Buenaventura, Main and Figueroa Streets, Ventura. Founded 1782

Santa Barbara, 2201 Laguna Street. Founded 1786

Santa Ynez, 1760 Mission Drive. Founded 1804

La Purísima Concepción, near Lompoc, off 101. Founded 1787

San Luis Obispo de Tolosa, Choro & Monterey Streets. Founded 1772

San Miguel Arcángel, 801 Mission Street. Founded 1797

San Antonio de Padua, off 101, Jolon. Founded 1771

Nuestra Señora de la Soledad, off Highway 101, 36641 Fort Romie Road. Founded 1791

Santa Clara de Asís, 500 El Camino Real. Founded 1777

San Carlos Borromeo de Carmelo, 3080 Rio Road Carmel. Founded 1770

San Juan Bautista, off Highway 101, 406 2nd Street. Founded 1797

Santa Cruz, 126 High Street. Founded 1791

In 1825 it had a population of 2,869 and, by 1832, a livestock herd of 57,380.

All of this came to a crashing end when the Mexican government, having won its independence from Spain in 1821, secularized the missions following its decree of August 9, 1834. The missions were never meant to last as huge land-owning entities. The churches would remain in the hands of the Franciscans, but the Mexican Secularization Laws moved the mission properties into private ownership. Indians were banished from what had been their homes, and the missions rapidly fell into ruin.

Mission San Miguel – "mission construction"

San José, 43300 Mission Boulevard, Fremont. Founded 1797

San Francisco de Asís (Mission Dolores), Dolores & 16th Street. Founded 1776

San Rafael Arcángel, 1104 Fifth Avenue. Founded 1817

San Francisco Solano de Sonoma, 363 3rd Street West. Founded 1823

EL CAMINO REAL — HIGHWAY 101 & THE ROUTE OF THE *DAYLIGHT*

Adobe & Earthquakes

Earthquakes were a great enemy of the missions. La Purisima was destroyed by the devastating quake of 1812. San Juan Capistrano was also devastated by the quake, as was Mission Santa Clara. It was so badly damaged the church had to be replaced. Mission Santa Barbara's bell towers and church were badly damaged by a 1925 earthquake that devastated the town. It was rebuilt with the Spanish flavor so in evidence today.

Simple neglect destroyed the majority of the missions following the Mexican secularization decree of 1834. The missions were generally either abandoned outright or sold to people who used them as stores, homes, or stables. The twenty-one missions, with few exceptions such as Santa Barbara and San Gabriel, were essentially nothing but a series of ruins. There was no effort to protect the fragile adobe walls by protecting the roof tiles. The tiles were stolen, and most of the adobe buildings melted into the earth. There was no resident priest from 1846 to 1933, but there were plenty of animals that had taken up residence in the former mission. Mission San Carlos Borromeo near Carmel fell to total ruin following secularization. Mission Soledad disappeared almost completely. Mission San Antonio suffered the same fate. La Purisima near Lompoc was equally devastated. Mission San Fernando was sold often, used as a barn, and became a complete ruin by the end of the nineteenth century.

Mission San Juan Capistrano ruins

Industrious Padres

Post cards depicting the industrious and self-sufficeint Padres of Santa Barbara Mission.

Shelling Peas for the Noonday meal, Santa Barbara Mission, Cal.

The Wood Cutters, Santa Barbara Mission, Cal.

When the Mexican government secularized the California missions in 1834, only one of them remained under the control of the Franciscan padres. Father Narciso Duran moved his headquarters as the president of the Alta California missions to Mission Santa Barbara in 1834 and California's first bishop, Francisco Garcia Diego y Moreno, moved his offices to Santa Barbara in 1840. The presence of the two leading Catholic churchmen in the territory caused Mexico to refrain from selling or trying to operate the Mission Santa Barbara church. By the time these post cards were printed in the 1908, the padres were doing most of the work at the mission. The ordained Franciscans were ably helped by the seminarians studying at the Mission.

An integral part of the clothing of all Franciscans is the St. Francis Cord worn at the waist. The founder of the order, St. Francis of Assisi, adopted the cord to symbolize his identification with the poor who commonly wore such a cord. Each cord has three knots in it, symbolizing the Franciscan's dedication to poverty, chastity, and obedience.

Making the St. Francis Cord, Santa Barbara Mission, Cal.

Flowers for the Altar, Santa Barbara Mission, Cal.

EL CAMINO REAL — HIGHWAY 101 & THE ROUTE OF THE *DAYLIGHT*

Mission San Juan Bautista – path of El Camino Real, 2011

In 1895, the missions came to the attention of Charles Fletcher Lummis, a lover of all things Spanish and a dedicated Southern California booster. He helped found the Landmarks Club in the same year and began to lobby aggressively to protect and save historic sites throughout the state of California, starting with the missions. Funding for the Landmarks Club came from private sources in America as well as around the world. The first project was Mission San Juan Capistrano south of Los Angeles. In northern California the California Historic Landmarks League was developed with a similar goal. The Native Sons and Daughters of the Golden West also became involved in the rescue of the missions early in the twentieth century. Later the Hearst Mission Restoration Fund was established in 1948 with an initial grant of $500,000. The money was distributed among the nineteen missions owned by the Catholic Church. The Hearst fund was particularly important to the salvation of Mission San Antonio de Padua, west of King City. The state of California wound up owning Mission La Purisima, which, by the 1930s, was a total ruin. The Civilian Conservation Corps rebuilt the mission, and the original route of El Camino Real.

Today, anyone traveling Highway 101 can visit all the missions in a restored state. Some notably Santa Barbara, San Juan Capistrano, San Gabriel, and the interior of Mission San

Miguel, are little changed from their original construction by the Indians and Franciscans. Others, such as Mission San Jose, Soledad, Santa Clara, San Diego, and San Fernando, had to be completely recreated according to the original plans. Mission Santa Cruz, rebuilt in 1933, is a smaller replica of the original church. The California missions are some of the most visited historic sites in the United States. All of them between Los Angeles and San Francisco are either right on or adjacent to Highway 101, the route of the padres.

El Camino Real was the only significant pathway in Alta California, and it connected not only the rungs on the ladder of missions but all the settlements and ranchos in that small part of the vast Spanish Empire. There would be re-routings of the original trail and numerous branch roads as the region developed. El Camino Real continued to evolve because it had to be the best and easiest route through the colony. Most of the people using it were walking. Ease of use was also a necessity because sea travel up the coast to Alta California from the colonial cities in Mexico was extremely difficult, given the prevailing winds and currents along the coast as well as the scarcity of Spanish ships in what was a backwater of the Spanish Empire.

There were any number of king's roads scattered among the Spanish colonies.

All the roads in a Spanish colony were owned by the king and, therefore, were royal roads. The Alta California Camino Real was not celebrated or remembered until Los Angeles boosters started looking for a past to celebrate for the insignificant, dusty, landlocked agricultural county seat they planned to make the biggest city in the United States. As the boosters warmed to their task in the 1890s, they knew finding additional sources of water was imperative since the Los Angeles River was almost tapped out and their landlocked town had to be connected to the ocean and an artificial harbor created. They

Scenes from *Ramona* outdoor play, staged annually at Hemet since 1923

EL CAMINO REAL — HIGHWAY 101 & THE ROUTE OF THE *DAYLIGHT*

also determined that a romantic past was needed to make their prosaic small town more interesting and more marketable.

The boosters were given a running start in romanticizing California's past by the phenomenal success of Helen Hunt Jackson's novel *Ramona* (published in 1884). She meant it to be an *Uncle Tom's Cabin* for California's Indians, but it was the doomed romance between the Indian Allessandro and the Scottish/Indian Ramona, who had been raised in luxury on the hacienda owned by Señora Moreno, that captured the audience. By the 1890s, the sites mentioned in the novel had become the first major tourist attractions in southern California. One of the key stops on the tour was on the old royal road, just off the Southern Pacific mainline through Ventura County. The Camulos Rancho was where Jackson did some of her research,

Scenes from *Ramona*

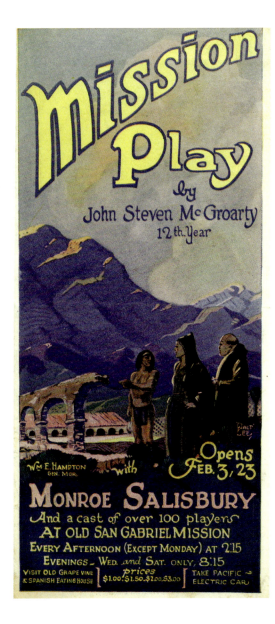

Mission Play, San Gabriel: Act 1 – "Baptism of the First Gentile"

Mission Play: Act 3 – "Señora Yorba's Lamentation"

and she used it as one of the models for Ramona's birthplace. The novel largely takes place as the Americans are occupying southern California. The days of Spanish control were portrayed nostalgically as an era of happiness and contentment.

But in the more than 600 pages of the novel there is not a single mention of El Camino Real. In the part where Felipe, Señora Moreno's son, went looking for Alessandro, he started in Monterey and traveled south on what Jackson described as "the route which the Franciscan Fathers used to take, when the only road on the California coast was the one leading from

Mission to Mission." When George Wharton James published *Through Ramona's Country* in 1908, he gave a name to that route. "El Camino Real – in plain English, the King's Highway – was the road, crude and primitive, that used to connect the old Missions from La Paz on the south, up the peninsula in Baja California, to San Diego in Alta California, and then on and up to Sonoma, where the last of the chain, San Francisco Solano, was located." James went on to endorse the effort to mark the path of the highway "for its practical and sentimental benefits" to both local farmers and the ever-growing number of tourists.

It took boosters like George Wharton James to bring back the name of the King's Highway and to push for its recognition. It was a part of their using the Spanish past as a way to glamorize California. Once the boosters got hold of the idea, the period of Spanish control was referred to as "The Days of the Dons." No one believed in it more fervently or prosely-

Broadway Cafeteria
422 SOUTH BROADWAY
A PLEASANT PLACE TO EAT
WHERE FOOD EXCELS
Dinner 3:00 P. M. to 7:45 P. M.
Specials That Will Surprise You
Be one of Our Boosters—Join Our Booster Club
ASK THE MANAGER
QUICK COURTEOUS SERVICE From 10:30 A. M. to 7:45 P. M.

The "California Catechism" is a 1912 post card from the Broadway Cafeteria in downtown Los Angeles. It is a perfect example of how dedicated the whole city was to the promotional "Booster" campaign being led by the chamber of commerce.

A typical chamber of commerce party with its members, "boosters" showing off their Spanish costumes. Los Angeles, 1922

BE A BOOSTER---CALIFORNIA CATECHISM

Question—Where is the State of California located?
Answer—On the front side of the American continent, between the rest of the United States and the Pacific Ocean, and near the Panama canal.
Q.—Why is Southern California famous?
A.—It contains Los Angeles.
Q.—What is Los Angeles?
A.—The climatic capital of the United States.
Q.—To what has it been likened?
A.—To paradise, heaven, Eden and the Riviera.
Q.—Which does it most resemble?
A.—It is a happy combination of all of them.
Q.—What is the population of Los Angeles?
A.—700,000 boosters (Will be more tomorrow).
Q.—What is a booster?
A.—One who knows a good thing and wants others to come and share it.
Q.—Of whom does the population consist?
A.—Mostly of people from Iowa, together with many former residents of other states and a sprinkling of native sons.
Q.—Into what two classes may the people of the United States be divided?
A.—Those who have already seen Southern California and those who intend to see it soon.
Q.—What are Eastern visitors called while visiting Los Angeles? A.—Tourists.
Q.—What is a tourist?
A.—A permanent resident in the bud.
Q.—What things may a tourist see in and around Los Angeles that he does not see back East?
A.—Oranges, ostriches, lemons, alligators, olives, missions, sardines, aqueducts, harbors, tunas, bungalows, abalones, loquats, cassaba melons, horned toads, snow-covered peaks, submarine gardens, yuccas, eucalyptus, palms, pepper trees, cafeterias, Thanksgiving celery and Christmas strawberries.
Q.—Does L. A. hide its light under a bushel?
A.—It does not. In addition to showing the light it sets fire to the bushel and makes a conflagration that attracts the attention of the whole world.
Q.—Has L. A. any agents working for it in the East?
A.—Yes. Mr. Cyclone, Mr. Blizzard, Mr. Thunderstorm and the two Wave brothers, Messrs. Cold and Hot.
Q.—Are they successful?
A.—Highly so. They are sending thousands of people to Los Angeles every year.
Q.—When is the best time to come to Los Angeles?
A.—At once. "Everybody's doing it."
Q.—What is the only way to leave Los Angeles?
A.—With a return ticket.
Q.—When will Los Angeles cease to exceed the speed limit in growing? A.—When Gabriel blows his horn.
Q.—Where is the best place to eat in Los Angeles?
A.—BROADWAY CAFETERIA.
422 S. Broadway Phone 614-51 Los Angeles
(Over)

tized it more enthusiastically than did the author of "The Mission Play," John Steven McGroarty. In his 1929 book, *Mission Memories*, the future poet laureate of California and United States congressman laid out a view of Spanish California that enthralled the boosters:

When the vast chain of twenty-one Missions was at last completed through the toiling and patient years, California was the happiest land the world has ever known. There was peace and plenty, and hospitality became a religion. The great oaken doors of the Missions swung inward with welcome to whomsoever might come…Song and laughter filled the sunny mornings. There was feasting and music, strum of guitars and the click of castanets under the low hanging moons.…

It was a sheer Utopia. Nothing like it ever existed before, nor has any approach to it existed since.

This kind of romantic yearning for the "Days of the Dons" and the King's Highway as its symbol was a long time coming. When Mexico took control of Alta California from the Spanish, it did not formally change the name, but the term "Royal

Highway" went out of favor in republican Mexico. When the Americans took control from the Mexicans, it was generally referred to as the Coast Route and never as, El Camino Real. Just as it was absent from *Ramona*, neither was it mentioned in the earliest railroad-produced booster guidebooks to southern California. It was absent from Charles Nordhoff's *California: A Book for Travellers and Settlers* (1873); Benjamin Truman's *Semi-Tropical California* (1874); Newton Chittenden's *Health and Pleasure Resorts of the Pacific Coast* (1884); Theodore Van Dyke's *Southern California: Its Valleys, Hills, and Streams* (1886); and Charles Dudley Warner's *Our Italy* (1891). It was not until historically minded boosters such as Charles Fletcher Lummis, Anna Pitcher, and Harrie (Mrs. A.S.C.) Forbes, grew interested in restoring the dilapidated missions that El Camino Real as the name of the historic route connecting them reentered the conversation.

Left: Don Josè Antonio Arillo

Right: Mission Santa Barbara, Old Spanish Days Fiesta

Mission San Fernando – El Camino Real in front with the Mission fountain to the right, ca 1900

Lummis, Pitcher, and Forbes convinced the Native Daughters of the Golden West, Landmarks Club, General Federation of Women's Clubs, El Camino Real Association of California, and the Los Angeles Chamber of Commerce to become engaged in and fund the task of mapping out the route of the former King's Highway and marking it properly.

Anna Pitcher got the idea to preserve the road in 1892. It took her a decade to drive the General Federation of Women's Clubs behind the issue. They directed their History and Landmarks Department, chaired by Harrie Forbes, to work with Pitcher to investigate and publicize El Camino Real.

Mission San Fernando restoration – making adobe bricks, ca 1920

EL CAMINO REAL — HIGHWAY 101 & THE ROUTE OF THE *DAYLIGHT*

Soon after her success, Anna Pitcher died. Harrie Forbes ably picked up her mantle. She would eventually persuade the Los Angeles Chamber of Commerce and Automobile Club of Southern California to help fund the project. The idea was to mark the route of El Camino Real, with a series of bells hanging from a shepherd's staff. Forbes is generally credited with the design of the bells and even made them in her foundry. The road the bells started to mark in 1906 was still quite primitive. But El Camino Real was finally returned to its rightful place as an icon in the history of California. All this work laid the groundwork for the Highway 101 we know today.

Below: Mission Santa Ynez, El Camino Real bell, 2012

Right: Mission San Luis Obispo dedication of El Camino Real bell, September 10, 1908

EL CAMINO REAL — HIGHWAY 101 & THE ROUTE OF THE *DAYLIGHT*

Mission Santa Ynez, Christopher Silva, Order of Capuchin Friars Minor, 2012

EL CAMINO REAL — HIGHWAY 101 & THE ROUTE OF THE *DAYLIGHT*

Chapter Two

Highway 101 in the Beginning

Highway 101 as a through, well-paved roadway connecting San Diego, Los Angeles, and San Francisco generally along the route of El Camino Real was a long time coming. What was commonly referred to as "the Coast Route" was originally the responsibility of towns near it to keep it at least passable. The California Legislature did not create the Bureau of Highways until 1895. At that time the only paved roads in the state were in cities and towns. Roads through rural areas were only slightly advanced from the days of the Franciscan padres. They seldom had signs and were only scarcely passable during the winter rains. As was common throughout the country in the nineteenth century, many of the few well-maintained and graded roads were privately owned and charged a toll. There were 159 toll roads in the loosely settled and underpopulated California prior to the dawn of the new century.

One of the first books dealing with the missions and how to get to them was A.C. Vroman's 1893 locally published *Mission Memories: The Franciscan Missions of California*. In the introduction, the Pasadena-based bookseller, photographer, and preservationist noted how to get to individual missions once a traveler arrived by train. He and a friend chose an alternative mode of travel when they spent two weeks in a horse-drawn wagon camping and seeing the missions on the road between Santa Barbara and San Francisco.

Left: *El Pasear* Auto Club members driving along El Camino Real in San Luis Obispo County, 1912

Above: Adam Clark Vroman on one of his travel adventures to photograph the 'Old West," 1904

An alternate route of El Camino Real climbed over the San Marcos Pass into the Santa Ynez Valley when the Gaviota Pass was blocked. The *Concord* stagecoach passengers posed for this picture at Hobo Rock, ca 1890

An alternate route of El Camino Real climbed over the Casitas Pass into Santa Barbara. Here at the top of Casitas Pass, Santa Barbara County, a White and a Mitchell auto stop at El Camino Real bell, 1906

Below: Rough road ahead for this Franklin Model G auto and driver; only three miles from Vernalis, in San Joaquin County, 1912

It was the constant demands of the growing number of "autoists" and the developing agricultural strength of the Coast Route towns that finally motivated state and local communities to improve the dirt paths that passed for roads in coastal California. The Mexican period (1821-46) had seen little change in the Royal Road. The name was not even changed to reflect the new rulers of California. The main change up and down El Camino Real was the secularization of the missions and subsequent release of the neophytes from the feudal system they were under. Mexico did nothing to help the Indians, who first lost their native way of life and then the mission life. They were abandoned.

American statehood did little to improve El Camino Real. The period between 1850 and 1860 was one of banditry along

AT&SF – American-type locomotive No. 328 (built in 1887 and scrapped in 1922)

the Coast Road. Its thin settlement and numerous ambush points made it a haven for highwaymen, such as Jack Powers, until the Vigilantes put an end to the robber gangs. The road was known simply as the coastal road between San Francisco and Los Angeles. Though a stage line finally connected the two cities in 1858, the pathway was ungraded and hills had to be climbed and descended as best as possible. There were no bridges, and any streams encountered required fording. Once a stagecoach or wagon reached Rincon Point near Ventura where the hills ran down to the sea, teamsters had to drive the team along the beach sand, and in the case of a higher tide, right through the surf. In stormy conditions travelers just had to wait.

By the time the Bureau of Highways became an official department of the state government in 1896, California was in a state of flux. Thanks to the connection of a new transcontinental route by the Santa Fe Railroad in 1885, competition broke out with the already established Southern Pacific Railroad. The rates to Los Angeles from Kansas City had been around $100. They soon began to fall rapidly, famously reaching $1.00 for

a few hours on March 6, 1887. The rate war led directly to the boom of the 1880s in the Los Angeles area that quadrupled the population. By 1890, the former "Queen of the Cow Counties" had a population of 50,395, paved streets, a streetcar line, and a chamber of commerce dedicated to making the agricultural center, then the country's 57th town in population, the biggest city in America. The chamber took aim at the same small farmers the railroads had been trying to lure for fifteen years. Many of those new immigrants explored the area around Los Angeles for a farm site and then headed north up the nascent Coast Highway to find land to their liking. The expanding agriculture of the region led to the necessity of proper transportation. The state finally started to respond in the 1890s.

The Los Angeles Consolidated Electric Railway car on the Westlake Park line entering Main Street from Spring in downtown Los Angeles, ca 1893

The twentieth century brought the mass-produced automobile and the need for paved roads. The ten-year-old Department of Highways became a division within the Department of Engineering in 1907. Three years later, California voters approved an $18 million bond issue for the construction of a state highway system. The first construction project broke ground on August 7, 1912, on a section of El Camino Real that connected San Francisco with Burlingame. It also saw the numbering of the roads that were called Legislative Routes. Route 2 would generally follow the Royal Road from San Diego to San Francisco.

Picking oranges, Los Angeles County, ca 1890

Main Street, Ventura Mission in the background on the left side, 1892

This earliest period of paving highways and building bridges along Route 2 saw the most aggressive work being started on its northern sections. San Francisco was still the major city in the state, and the Santa Clara Valley with San Jose as its leading city was well established as a canning and shipping center. The next stop was the fishing port of Monterey and the agricultural center of Salinas. Roads started snaking out of Los Angeles to the wheat fields of the San Fernando Valley and south to the new federally funded harbor at San Pedro and on to the natural harbor at San Diego. Santa Barbara was already established as a resort by the early twentieth century, and several paved roads left that city to the surrounding countryside.

Driver in a 1911 Franklin Model G auto costing $2,150, seems confused by all the signs, a short distance from Monterey, 1912

EL CAMINO REAL — HIGHWAY 101 & THE ROUTE OF THE *DAYLIGHT*

Newly paved two-lane Coast Highway at Rincon, ca 1920

Construction of the nearly completed Santa Ynez River Bridge, 1918

By the 1920s, road building across the country was becoming a standardized process. California was an aggressive part of the new highway construction booming across the United States. Most of the gaps on Route 2 had been filled in along the Coast Route by this time. A well-graded concrete roadbed had replaced the original wooden highway around Rincon Point. Bridges crisscrossed the Salinas River down through the Valley. The Gaviota Pass had been widened to allow the passage of two automobiles side by side. The highway was changed from running east around the Nojoqui Grade to Solvang and Mission Santa Ynez to a more direct route over the Santa Ynez River through the new town of Buellton and on to Santa Maria. In 1922 this was the last part of Route 2 to be paved.

For some time the American Association of State Highway Officials had been concerned with the haphazard growth and directions of the named highway system of that era. That organization was formed in 1914 with the goal of helping to establish

Cuesta Grade's curves were widened and a reinforced concrete pavement was put down, 1922

national roadway standards. The two most famous of the existing national roads were the Lincoln Highway and the National Old Trails Highway. The association's concern was the lack of engineering logic behind the direction the national roads took. They often reflected an odd jog because a town had paid to be included on the road. Plus the signage of the roads was often a simple notice painted on a tree or utility pole. On March 2, 1925, the association appointed a Joint Board on Interstate Highways. There was bitter opposition from some of the existing auto trail associations as well as from local and states rights groups. Nonetheless, on November 11, 1926, the plan to inaugurate the United States Highway system was approved by the association. Among the first routes were Highway 101 connecting San Diego, Los Angeles, and San Francisco along the path of the Alta California missions and the former California Route 2.

Cuesta Grade – SLOW, ca 1912

Cuesta Grade Summit – Upper Lopez Canyon – Highway 101 sign carved on a wooden plank, ca 1912

San Fernando Valley from Chalk Hills near Pierce College, 1923

Ruined walls of Mission La Purisima, Lompoc, 2011

Meanwhile back on the Coast Route, much had already been done to link the soon to be replaced State Legislative Route 2 with the historic El Camino Real. All the way back in 1902, Anna Pitcher had proposed revitalizing the route of the padres to the California Federation of Women's Clubs and the Native Daughters of the Golden West. She, along with Charles Fletcher Lummis, George Wharton James, Harrie (Mrs. A.S.C.) Forbes, and Christine Sterling, were concerned with celebrating the Spanish past of the state. While Sterling chiefly concerned herself with resurrecting the original plaza in Los Angeles, the other four concentrated on honoring El Camino Real and rebuilding the Franciscan missions that were largely only ruins by the turn of the twentieth century. To this end the El Camino Real Association was founded in 1904 to research the route of the original road and decide where to put the signs.

Coast Highway countryside with unique perforated bell sign, ca 1912

The signs were a very important development. Roads in California, such as they were in the new century, tended to be a guessing game. Local entities did little to let motorists either know where they were or how to get on to the next stop on what passed for the road. Starting in 1914, the Automobile Club of Southern California took up the task of putting up road signs around the state. That lasted into the post-World War II era, when state and local governments finally assumed the role.

But El Camino Real was a unique story. The El Camino Real Association was good to its word.

Harrie Forbes is usually credited with designing the bell and staff marker that was to be placed along the route. In her 1915 book on El Camino Real, she explained the design motif used for the road markers. Forbes said she used a bell for the road marker because "at all times the padres first hung a bell that they might call attention to the work in hand, that of erect-

El Camino Real bell with verdant agricultural fields, 2011

Right: Mrs. A.S.C. Forbes in her bell factory, ca 1925

EL CAMINO REAL — HIGHWAY 101 & THE ROUTE OF THE *DAYLIGHT*

Calabasas, Oak Garage named for hangman's oak tree. El Camino bell—21 miles to Mission San Fernando, 43 miles to Mission San Buenaventura, 1936

ing and blessing the cross." The bell and staff were to be made of iron, which was selected "for the reason that the entire proposition to reconstruct El Camino Real is intended to represent the iron will of the men who made the first roads in California." The first bell was placed with much fanfare at the Plaza Church in downtown Los Angeles on August 15, 1906.

Forbes not only led in the effort to mark El Camino Real and in the design of the bells, but in 1914 her husband started the California Bell Factory and started making both the bells to be used on the highway as well as souvenir bells to raise money for the great project. Harrie took over running the factory on her husband's death in 1928. The original idea was to put a bell about a mile apart along the route between San Diego and San Francisco. County and local laws did not always make this possible, but the coast route from San Diego to San Francisco—and all the missions in between—was

EL CAMINO REAL — HIGHWAY 101 & THE ROUTE OF THE *DAYLIGHT*

Coast Highway 101 near Rincon, ca 1932

clearly marked for the first time. There were few other signposts on the road. Following the bells became the only way to know how to reach to the next mission in the ladder.

Highway 101 has been a work in progress for over a century. The first task was to make sure a paved road with manageable grades and curves, proper signage, and adequate bridges was in place. All of that was accomplished by the end of the 1920s. During the 1930s, the roadbed was improved regarding the grading and curves encountered on the highway. During World War II, gas and tire rationing cut down severely on civilian traffic. But the Coast Route became one of the leading military highways in the country. Military camps and ports were located up and down the highway. Convoys of troops and materiel were daily sights on the wartime 101. Once the war was over, widening became the issue due to the enormous increase in tourist travel, burgeoning use of trucks, and the marked growth of the many towns served by the 101.

Line of military wagons descending the Cuesta Grade, ca 1905

Further updates began to affect both the direction and size of the 101 in the late 1940s. The two ends of the route became freeways. The stretch through the Cahuenga Pass out to the San Fernando Valley became the Hollywood Freeway. The section running between Redwood City and South San Francisco became the Bay Area's first freeway. The process continued over the next twenty years until the stretches between Redwood City and San Jose were upgraded to freeway. In 1964 what used to be the 101 bypass was realigned to become the Bayshore Freeway that connected to the Bay Bridge in San Francisco.

One of the biggest changes in the 101 occurred down south when the old highway disappeared into Interstate 5 between

Cahuenga Pass with its Pacific Electric right-of-way at the Mulholland Highway stop; note the underground tunnel entrance for passengers, 1948

Opposite: Aerial of downtown Los Angeles – Hollywood Freeway transition to the San Ana Freeway, 1952

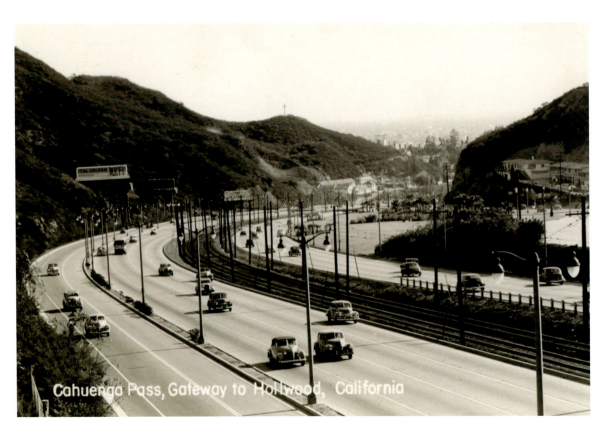

EL CAMINO REAL — HIGHWAY 101 & THE ROUTE OF THE *DAYLIGHT*

Spring Street, Paso Robles was Highway 101 before freeway bypassed the town, 2012

Monterey Street, Gilroy was Highway 101 before Freeway bypassed the town, 2012

El Camino Real four-lane highway beside older two-lane 101, 2011

Los Angeles and San Diego in 1966. By the 1960s and 1970s, the plan to bypass as many of the towns as possible was carried out. Monterey Street in Gilroy and Spring Street in Paso Robles were two of the former routes of the 101 that became just city streets when the main highway was moved outside the towns. This was also the era of ensuring that the entire length of the 101 was at least a four-lane highway. It is still not an Interstate highway since there are at-grade level cross roads in some parts north of Santa Barbara. The last stop signs on the 101–the four signal lights at Santa Barbara–were not bypassed until 1992. That was truly the end of an era. Highway 101 became a multi-laned, free-of-signals roadway for its entire length between Los Angeles and San Francisco. But the geographic realities of the route ensure that it will always at least flirt with the towns on its route and never be the anonymous, albeit rapid, roadway to be found farther east on Interstate 5.

Aerial of Highway 101 between Pismo Beach and Arroyo Grande, 1956

Wooden planked causeway near Rincon Point opened November 1, 1912

The Cuesta Grade descent to San Luis Obispo, ca 1923

Construction on the Coast Highway at Rincon Point, ca 1915

HIGHWAY ENGINEERING
Cuesta Grade – Rincon Point – Gaviota Pass

The three great impediments to the construction of Highway 101 were the Cuesta Grade north of San Luis Obispo, Rincon Point just north of Ventura, and Gaviota Pass, north of Santa Barbara, where the highway turns inland from the Pacific Ocean.

Conquering the Cuesta was a matter of automobiles being able to ascend an eight-mile long upgrade of switchbacks and steep grades.

At Rincon Point, the impediment was the hills extending down to the ocean shoreline. Enough of the hill had to be excavated to build a highway around the point, once it became evident that the wooden-causeway, built in 1912 and used until 1924, was not a feasible solution.

EL CAMINO REAL — HIGHWAY 101 & THE ROUTE OF THE *DAYLIGHT*

Early path through the Gaviota Pass, ca 1870

Early road through the Gaviota Pass, ca 1920

The Gaviota Pass highway widening has been a work in progress for well over a century. After a rainstorm, it would often be filled in by debris, which required a laborious cleaning by man and horse. When Gaviota Pass was closed, the travelers were forced to divert to the steep climb over San Marcos Pass. The first effort at widening Gaviota Pass was to trim the joining of the hills to allow a fully loaded wagon or stagecoach to pass through in 1861. It was further expanded for the automobile to allow two lanes of traffic to fit through in 1915, when the road was still officially State Legislative Route 2. In 1953, this was expanded to four lanes by boring through the 420-foot-long Gaviota Pass Tunnel for the two northbound lanes while the old highway became the southbound lanes. The rock and mudslides that accompany rain are as prevalent now as in the nineteenth century. This has caused Caltrans to install a series of nets through the pass to decrease erosion and prevent falling rocks from blocking the roadway.

Gaviota Pass Tunnel, Highway 101 northbound lanes, 2012

EL CAMINO REAL — HIGHWAY 101 & THE ROUTE OF THE *DAYLIGHT*

PORTFOLIO: **EL PASEAR**

An Automobile Trip Along State Legislative Route 2

El Pasear – Santa Maria Garage, Santa Barbara County, 1912

The Panama Canal was scheduled to open in 1915. That event would have an obvious and major impact on the ports of the West Coast. In a California already gripped by the booster spirit, this was a cause for huge celebrations. Two significant fairs were to be held at the homes of the largest natural harbors in the state. The San Diego Panama-Pacific International Exposition was designed to put the small southern city on the map. The similarly named expo in San Francisco was to be a true world's fair as befitted the leading harbor and city in California.

A group of highway boosters in Inyo County under the leadership of W. Gillette Scott recognized an opportunity when they heard about it. A tie-in with the San Francisco fair would not only publicize their area; it would also help in the good roads campaign that would make their remote part of California more accessible. A letter was written to Governor Hiram Johnson proposing funding for what the Inyo County Good Roads Club called "El Pasear Tour." With a nod to the fabled Spanish past, pasear means to walk, loiter, or look around.

El Pasear – Mission San Carlos Borromeo de Carmelo 1912

PORTFOLIO: El Pasear

The governor agreed to fund their venture with further sponsorship by the Automobile Club of California. The Pasear route proposed to take four cars along El Camino Real from San Francisco, through Los Angeles, and on to San Diego. After returning to Los Angeles, the motorists would head east across the Mojave Desert and north to Lake Tahoe, and on to Sacramento and back to San Francisco. The trip would encompass more than 2,000 miles and travel through twenty-two California counties.

El Pasear was designed to show visitors an alternative way to get to the upcoming fair, publicize the need for improving the state's highways, and support the "See America First" movement. But it also had the role of promoting the wonders of Inyo County and the rest of California to all Americans. As the Los Angeles Times noted on October 20, 1912, "Without doubt the completion of the Pasear will do much to promote touring in the West. Taking in as it does every climatic condition from the cold of the snow-clad Sierras to the extreme heat of the Mojave desert, and embracing soil which produces everything from the orange and rose to sage brush and cacti, the route is typical of the land of perpetual promise."

The Pasear motorists left San Francisco's Palace Hotel on June 10, 1912. For the next month they leisurely explored the state in four EMF (Everitt-Metzger-Flanders) touring cars. The company, often derided with claims its initials stood for "Every Morning Fix It" or "Every Mechanical Fault," was already under the wing of the Studebaker Corporation and would be bought outright the following year. The cars were donated by the San Francisco branch of Studebaker and set out under the Pasear slogan, "The highway with a thousand byways – each byway with a thousand wonders." Local boosters along the way joined the EMF's. Photographers from the McCurry Foto Company, Sacramento's leading commercial photography house captured the entire journey on 8 x 10 glass negative plates.

The Pasear journey bore fruit. The state's newspapers and national magazines extensively covered the trip, and the McCurry photographs were widely distributed. The first state highway construction project to pave State Legislative Route 2 from San Francisco to Burlingame was let to contract on July 23, 1912, two weeks after the Pasear motorists so clearly highlighted the primitive nature of California's highways. By the time the Panama-Pacific International Exposition opened in February 1915, the state highway system had begun the long process of challenging the railroad as the principal means of moving people in California.

El Pasear – Andrews Hotel, San Luis Obispo, 1912

PORTFOLIO: El Pasear

74

El Pasear – Jolon Grade, Monterey County, 1912

PORTFOLIO: El Pasear

El Pasear – Pismo Hotel, San Luis Obispo County, 1912

PORTFOLIO: El Pasear

El Pasear – Supply Car on Pismo Beach, San Luis Obispo County, 1912

El Pasear – Hotel Potter, Santa Barbara, 1912

PORTFOLIO: El Pasear

PORTFOLIO: El Pasear

El Pasear – The wood-planked Rincon Coast Route near Ventura, 1912

PORTFOLIO: El Pasear

PORTFOLIO: El Pasear

El Pasear – San Buenaventura Mission, Ventura, 1912

PORTFOLIO: El Pasear

El Pasear – San Gabriel Mission, San Gabriel, 1912

PORTFOLIO: El Pasear

Chapter Three
Daylight

The Route of the *Daylight*

The most famous train of the Southern Pacific's "Route of the Padres" was the streamlined *Coast Daylight*, which ran under steam and later diesel between San Francisco and Los Angeles from 1937 to 1955. Called "The most beautiful train in the World," it was the hallmark of California's coastal transportation when the American railroad system was at its apex in the 1920s, '30s, and '40s. The gleaming result of a statewide rail system, however, was a long time coming.

California is not an easy place in which to build railroads. The most significant valleys in the state run north and south, but even relatively flat terrain is crossed by dozens of small, winter-swollen streams requiring expensive bridging, cuts, and fills. The valleys are also broken by several pesky east-west mountain ranges that could be overcome only with tunnels, and dramatic engineering feats, such as the famous Tehachapi Loop. The state's original north-south railroad line, branching off the transcontinental railroad near Stockton to run through the San Joaquin Valley to southern California, was begun in 1870 and took six years to build. Twenty-four years would pass until a parallel "Coast Route" was completed.

In fact, a line that followed the old Camino Real began with the fifty-mile San Francisco and San Jose Railroad, which connected those two cities and commenced full service on January 16, 1864.

The *Daylight* No. 4449 crossing the Gaviota trestle, June 19, 1984

Right: Steel blue rails over the Gaviota trestle, 2011

Tehachapi Loop tracks wind around Walong

Southern Pacific Railroad Depot, San Jose, ca 1908

California has never lacked for dreamers. San Franciscans had spoken of a coastal rail line to southern California from the early 1850s, but real progress did not occur until visionaries could be found in individuals who possessed the energy, political skills, and financial resources to make things happen. Such men were Sacramento businessmen Collis P. Huntington, Leland Stanford, Mark Hopkins, and Charles Crocker, creators of the Central Pacific Railroad, the western half of the transcontinental railroad that Congress had authorized and President Abraham Lincoln had signed into law in 1862. Having completed this line across the Sierras linking San Francisco with the Union Pacific at Promontory, Utah, in 1869, the "Big Four" (as they were later known) began to explore the prospects for building southward in California.

Between March and November 1870, a Southern Pacific survey party led by Butler Ives conducted a horseback reconnaissance along the California coast south of San Jose. In 1872, Huntington and his associates became concerned that the New York-based Atlantic & Pacific Railroad would build through this same area as a result of a federal charter it had received. To forestall such a move, they incorporated a "Southern Pacific Branch Railroad" in December of 1872, a portion of

Portraits of the four founders of the Central Pacific and the Southern Pacific Railroads were painted by Stephen William Shaw (American, 1817-1900). The portraits are oil on canvas, 30 x 25 inches. E.B. Crocker Collection, Crocker Art Museum

Leland Stanford, 1874

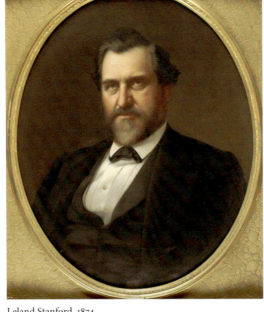

Mark Hopkins, 1873

Collis P. Huntington, 1874

Charles Crocker, 1874

"Driving the Golden Spike" – re-creation from the motion picture *Union Pacific* Paramount, 1939

Atlantic & Pacific Railroad locomotive No. 95, ca 1890

EL CAMINO REAL — HIGHWAY 101 & THE ROUTE OF THE *DAYLIGHT*

Side-hill Harvesting with a Caterpillar.

which was projected to follow the coast as far south as Ventura. The following summer, Southern Pacific President Collis P. Huntington traveled this line by stagecoach from Los Angeles to the railhead at Soledad in the Salinas Valley. Although the line to Soledad went into operation on August 12, 1872, the associates decided to suspend work at that point. With the threat of the Atlantic & Pacific fading, the Southern Pacific spent its capital on building its southern transcontinental route to New Orleans, an expensive undertaking not completed until 1883. Another three years passed before work on the Coast Line finally resumed.

The "Boom of the '80s" established Los Angeles as a growing city and fed competition between the Southern Pacific and the newly arrived Atchison, Topeka & Santa Fe Railway. A major rate war broke out between the two companies, and thousands of Americans took advantage of the cheap fares to explore southern California.

Enough of them stayed to expand the agricultural base of Los Angeles and demand better transportation for the entire region. New rail lines were built to bring the wheat, wine, and citrus crops of the San Fernando Valley into the city. The boom also added impetus to the Coast Line effort, with train service beginning between Santa Barbara and Los Angeles opening on August 20, 1887.

In October 1888, the Southern Pacific resumed work on the northern branch and reached Santa Margarita three months later. But the boom had run its course, and southland real estate values plummeted. Short of cash and confronted by the difficult Santa Lucia Mountains north of San Luis Obispo, the railroad chose once again to wait. No progress occurred

Santa Margarita (north of San Luis Obispo), Hotel Margarita adjacent to the Santa Margarita Land Company, ca 1910

for another three years. The Southern Pacific was spurred to action a few years later when both the Union Pacific and the Santa Fe Railroads, acting through surrogates, began to make moves from the east to the California Coast. In those circumstances, Huntington came to San Luis Obispo in April of 1889 and suggested that construction to close the gap could begin again within a year.

But there was a catch. The line through the Santa Lucias, Huntington explained to a group of civic leaders and ranchers, was going to be expensive. He promised that construction would begin within a year if the company were granted free right of way, station grounds, and a $300,000 subsidy. The citizens of the coastal counties, recognizing the financial and transportation benefits the railroad would bring, agreed to raise the money. They did so.

Work began again in October 1891, south of Santa Margarita. It took three more years to complete the seventeen miles to penetrate the Santa Lucia Range and reach San Luis Obispo. In the process, seven tunnels were bored through the mountains and a great loop, even larger than that at Tehachapi was built on a huge earthen berm. The 80-foot-high bridge over Stenner Creek posed particular difficulties. Parts of the bridge were made in Pittsburgh and had to be shipped to the site from Pennsylvania; pieces of the structure disappeared in transit, some of which were found on a siding in New Orleans. Eventually, the trestle pieces were riveted into place, track-laying was completed, and the first train whistled into San Luis Obispo on May 5, 1894.

Construction crews continued on for another fifty miles of track south of San Luis Obispo until work as far south as Surf (near modern-day Lompoc) was completed on August 18, 1896. But it was not until March 20, 1904, that the Coast Line was completed.

To accommodate larger and heavier trains, major improvements were still needed. Trackage between San Francisco to San Jose was upgraded, including the additional double track between San Jose to San Bruno. A new Bayshore Cutoff eliminated the steep, curving ascent over the shoulder of Mount San Bruno that had long plagued Southern Pacific operations into San Francisco. The cutoff required a great deal of cutting and filling, five tunnels, and a massive trestle, and wound up

Stenner Creek Bridge in the Santa Lucia Mountain Range, Cuesta Grade, north of San Luis Obispo, ca 1890

Southern Pacific railroad depot, San Luis Obispo, ca 1890

Bayshore Cutoff – Caltrain approaching from tunnel No. 4 at the San Francisco city limit, 2009

Montalvo Cutoff – The West End powerhouse supplied electricity and air ventilation for excavating Tunnel No. 26 in the Santa Susana Pass, ca 1900

The Southern Pacific reached Paso Robles on October 31, 1886

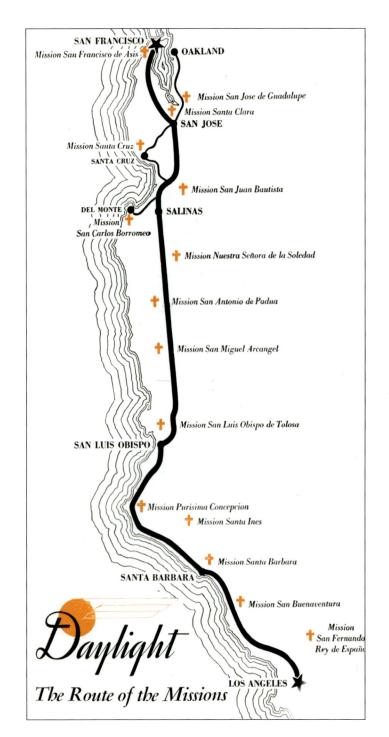

The *Daylight*, locomotive No. 4428, Train 99 readied to leave for San Francisco from the Los Angeles Union Passenger Terminal, ca 1940

Opposite: *Daylight* train No. 99, locomotive No. 4428 – Santa Susanna Pass – west of Chatsworth, April 1939

costing $1 million per mile. At the southern end of the Coast Line, no fewer than eighteen line changes were made, the most significant being the Montalvo Cutoff. The resulting line connecting the Simi and San Fernando Valleys by way of Santa Susanna Pass reduced curvature and grades, thereby saving time and effort on the part of the railroad. The new route improved freight revenues considerably by allowing the large sugar beet crops from the Imperial Valley to be shipped to processing plants in Oxnard and Betteravia.

Passenger service, however, was the main beneficiary of the new connection. "But what a scenic route it will be!" the Santa Barbara *Morning Press* predicted on December 6, 1898.

EL CAMINO REAL — HIGHWAY 101 & THE ROUTE OF THE *DAYLIGHT*

"Twelve hours from Los Angeles to San Francisco, and no heat, little dust, and no ferrying! O Yum!" The Coast Route, with its magnificent vistas and pleasant summer temperatures, soon hosted a half-dozen name trains. Year after year, hundreds of thousands of travelers enjoyed this engineering and scenic wonder. It was no surprise when, in 1937, the Southern Pacific chose the Coast Route to run its *Daylight* streamliner with powerful special steam locomotives built by Lima Locomotive Works of Ohio and new lightweight passenger cars. The entire train, painted in a stunning California red, orange, and black scheme, was a welcome winner during the Great Depression.

The *Daylight* was a true high-speed train. It was able to cruise along at an average of 70 miles per hour pulling fourteen streamlined passenger cars with an average running time between Los Angeles and San Francisco of nine hours and thirty minutes. In Los Angeles the *Daylight* began its historic operation on March 21, 1937, from the Southern Pacific Central Station located at Fifth Street and Central Avenue. In order for the train to reach its San Francisco destination, it had to travel along Alameda Street, already in the 1930s a busy business thoroughfare. That changed in 1939, when the Los Angeles Union Passenger Terminal (LAUPT) was opened and

Above: The *Daylight* speeds along the Pacific Ocean at Sacate siding north of Santa Barbara, ca 1940

Opposite: Central Station used by both the Southern Pacific and the Union Pacific Railroads with a Los Angeles Railway streetcar running in front of station, ca 1930

EL CAMINO REAL — HIGHWAY 101 & THE ROUTE OF THE *DAYLIGHT*

Arriving on schedule into Los Angeles at 6:00 p.m., the *Coast Daylight* being pulled by locomotive No. 4459, 1948

The *Daylight*, locomotive No. 4424, Train 98 arrival in Los Angeles running along Alameda Street on its way to the Central Station, May 1939

Opposite: *Daylight* running beside Highway 101, between Santa Barbara and Ventura heading toward Los Angeles. Multi-lane highway in the background and the early two-lane road in the foreground, ca 1945

EL CAMINO REAL — HIGHWAY 101 & THE ROUTE OF THE *DAYLIGHT*

EL CAMINO REAL — HIGHWAY 101 & THE ROUTE OF THE *DAYLIGHT*

The *Daylight*, locomotive No. 4428, Train 99 taking on water in Santa Barbara on its way to San Francisco, ca 1940

all Southern Pacific passenger trains could depart from there. The Southern Pacific always had the monopoly for its trains to terminate in downtown San Francisco, arriving and departing from Third and Townsend Streets. Today, this area south of Market Street has become a trendy part of downtown.

The *Daylight* train was so successful for the Southern Pacific that additional ones had to be added during the day to accommodate its passengers. Train No. 98 left San Francisco at 8:15 a.m. sharp every morning of the week. It made only five stops along the way. The first occurred at 9:08 a.m. in San Jose, followed at 10:36 a.m. in Salinas and 1:11 p.m. in San Luis Obispo, which was the halfway point on the trip. Both the northbound and southbound *Daylights* met just north of town. From San Luis Obispo the train sailed mostly along the coast all the way to

8:00 a.m. *Daylight* GS-4 No. 4444 brings *The Coaster* from San Francisco into the Los Angeles Union Station, 1948

8:15 a.m. The *Morning Daylight* pulls out of track No. 8 for San Francisco from the Los Angeles Union Station. The United State Post Office Terminal Annex can be seen in the background, 1948

Oxnard 156 miles south. The next stop after San Luis Obispo was Santa Barbara. Then came Glendale, and the train pulled into Los Angeles at 6:00 p.m. for a total of 470 miles from San Francisco. Glendale, only twenty minutes from the Los Angeles terminus, was mainly for celebrities to disembark, usually enabling them to avoid newspaper reporters and photographers. How much did this ride cost? Exactly $6.00 one-way!

Within three years of the *Daylight*'s inaugural run, a second *Daylight* was added to the daily roster. That train left at noon and arrived in San Francisco at 9:40 p.m. traveling over the same scenic coastal route.

Only one year later, on July 4, 1941, the *San Joaquin Daylight* was inaugurated between Oakland, through the San Joaquin Valley and over the Tehachapi Pass, and into Los Angeles.

EL CAMINO REAL — HIGHWAY 101 & THE ROUTE OF THE *DAYLIGHT*

Daylight GS-5, No. 4458, the first of two locomotives with roller bearings, Train 98 north of San Jose, 1943

Daylight GS-4 No. 4451, Train 98 highballing toward Los Angeles through a eucalyptus grove near Arroyo Grande, ca 1945

Finally, one more train was added, a deluxe, all-room sleeping-car streamliner between San Francisco and Los Angeles called the *Lark*. It was a first-class night train popular with business people leaving Los Angeles and/or San Francisco at 9:00 p.m. with its arrival at 9:00 a.m., in time for a business day.

Looking back at the *Daylight* advertising phrases – *Finer! Faster! 7,000,000 Passengers Can't be Wrong! Atmosphere of Luxury! The World's Most Beautiful Trains!* – we wonder if they were exaggerating. No! We cannot imagine the speed and splendor of those trains. They had to be experienced, and even though an original *Daylight* locomotive and some *Daylight* cars have been preserved, they can no longer travel at the 70 miles per hour along the Coast Route, as they did on that March day in 1937.

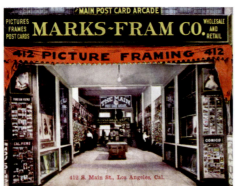

THE "LOS ANGELES SPECIAL"

Main Street in downtown Los Angeles in the early twentieth century was home to retail stores of all kinds, theaters showing three movies for a dime, tattoo parlors, inexpensive restaurants, bars with entertainment, and most of the remaining burlesque shows in the city. One of the many small shops on Main Street was at 412, next to James Lankershim's San Fernando Building. It was home to an elaborate mock-up of a train with a sign over the rear platform saying "Los Angeles Special." Such mock-ups were a staple of the pre-World War I tourist industry. A few doors south of the "train," you could have your picture taken with an "orange tree." The most unusual thing about the train at 412 Main Street was how long it lasted. Visitors were happily posing on its platform from shortly after the turn of the century until the post-World War II era. The train at 412 was originally in the Marks-Fram Company's post card and photo arcade. By 1920, the storefront was home to Stephen Soldi's Photo Studio. Then 412 and the storefronts around it were torn down in the mid-1930s. The train was moved a block north to the postcard emporium/gift shop run by Soldi's brother Vincent at 316 Main Street. The "Los Angeles Special" ran from the dawn of aviation into the atomic age. Quite a trip!

EL CAMINO REAL — HIGHWAY 101 & THE ROUTE OF THE *DAYLIGHT*

EL CAMINO REAL — HIGHWAY 101 & THE ROUTE OF THE *DAYLIGHT*

EL CAMINO REAL — HIGHWAY 101 & THE ROUTE OF THE *DAYLIGHT*

Chapter Four

Three Towns: Bradley, San Miguel, and Buellton

Highway 101 used to run right down the middle of Bradley, San Miguel, and Buellton. The first two small towns are in Monterey County near Camp Roberts. Buellton is further south in the northern part of Santa Barbara County. All three began life as agricultural towns and were closely united with the development of Highway 101 in the 1920s. But their fates could not be more different. It is a story of either having a built-in attraction or creating one. San Miguel had its mission. Buellton became home to the "Pea Soup" Andersen restaurant and numerous gas stations and motels at a crossroads to two missions. Bradley had none of these things. San Miguel and Buellton survived the realignment of 101 outside their towns and gradually prospered. Bradley did not.

Bradley was always the smallest of the three towns. It was founded in 1886 and named for Bradley Sargent, who owned the land on which the train station was built. It was never much of a passenger stop for the Southern Pacific, but the station was kept busy shipping cattle and produce. When the 101 was connected in the early 1920s, Bradley became another service town along the route. Several gas stations and lunch counters sprang up and the 1945 edition of the *California Mission Trails* booklet suggested Allen's Motel at $3.00 a night as a place to pause for the night.

Aerial view of Andersen's Pea Soup complex, Buellton, ca 1946

Bradley – abandoned gas station and chicken coop, 2012

Below: Bradley Catholic Church on Highway 101 before freeway bypassed town, 2012

The main role Bradley played on 101 was as the place to turn off the highway to catch the Jolan Road that eventually took you to Mission San Antonio from the south. Parallel highway and railroad bridges brought trains and cars from the west side of the Salinas River to Bradley's location on the east side. That changed when the 101 was widened and straightened in the 1960s. Bradley was bypassed. It was no longer a service town. One by one all the small businesses aimed at the motoring trade closed down. By the beginning of the twenty-first century, the population had dropped to 120 and residents had to do their shopping elsewhere. The only functioning businesses in town are the Catholic Church on the southern end; and the post office, the Bradley Forest Fire Station, and the Department of Forestry and Fire Protection of the State of California on the northern end.

San Miguel is the next town south of Bradley, about 10 miles down the 101. It is a mission town dating to 1797. Mission San Miguel was the sixteenth built in the chain and had been one of the more successful. The Southern Pacific established a station in 1886, once again with the emphasis on the

Mission San Miguel, 2012

EL CAMINO REAL — HIGHWAY 101 & THE ROUTE OF THE *DAYLIGHT*

San Miguel's Southern Pacific depot, 1886

California's Mission Trails Guide, ca 1948

San Miguel Shady Rest Motel cabins, 2011

shipment of agricultural products, rather than passengers. The typical service businesses cropped up, with gas stations located on either end of town as well as in the center. The *Mission Trails* guide had several suggestions for the traveler looking for a bed for the night. There were two hotels, the Mission and the Casa Blanca. The San Miguel Motel was also available, as was the Shady Rest, which noted, "We're from South Dakota. Where are you from?" If you needed a malted milk on a hot day, you had the choice of Larson's Garage and Soda Fountain or Chames Fountain opposite the train station.

This increase in choices is indicative of what saved San Miguel even after the 101 left town after its widening. The town had a well-preserved mission. It was a built-in tourist attraction that had the distinction of being, as John Steven McGroarty noted, a familiar sight to both "passengers on the railway trains and automobiles on the State Highway." Another advantage was that the bypass was not separated from the town by the Salinas River. The 101 is only scores of yards away from the town. The mission is plainly visible from the highway. In fact it is the one place the railroad, the highway, and a mission are next to each other. Most of the service entities in town have closed or changed, but San Miguel sports a new housing development on its north end. It is no threat to King City as the dominant town in the southern part of the Salinas Valley, but

EL CAMINO REAL — HIGHWAY 101 & THE ROUTE OF THE *DAYLIGHT*

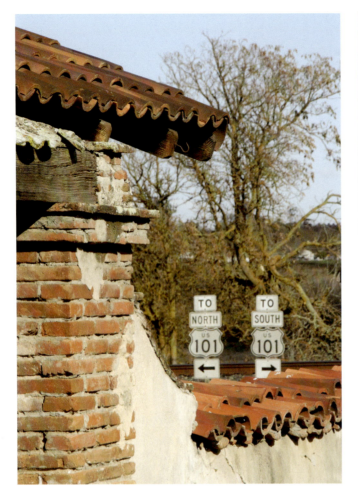

Mission San Miguel directional 101 signs, 2012

Coast Starlight viewed from Mission San Miguel archway, 2012

San Miguel restaurant and market signs, 2011

EL CAMINO REAL — HIGHWAY 101 & THE ROUTE OF THE *DAYLIGHT*

Construction of bridge over the Santa Ynez Creek leading to Buellton, 1917

it is prospering due to the continued presence of Mission San Miguel – which led to the Mission Market and Deli, Mission Drug Store, Mission Variety Store, Mission Restaurant, and Mission Pizza.

Buellton is in northern Santa Barbara County. It is the first town reached after leaving the Pacific Ocean and heading past Refugio and Gaviota, and navigating the Pass and the hills beyond it as you head north on 101. This was a new route for the Coast Highway, which formerly ran through Solvang and was the last part to be paved in 1922. A bridge was built over the Santa Ynez River, and starting in 1920 a town was created out of one part of R.T. Buell's Ranch, which had been divided among his sons into seven sections. Buellton quickly became a shipping point for cattle and milk products, but it was also in a perfect location for the mission-inspired tourist trade. The 1939 WPA Guide to California noted the town is called "the Mission Cross Roads" since it was where California Highway 246 intersected with Highway 101. The 246 connected Buellton with two

Flower fields near Lompoc, 2012

Solvang, "The Scandinavian Capital of America," 2012

towns and two missions. To the west lay the vast flower fields of Lompoc and Mission La Purisima. To the east lay the Danish capital of America, Solvang and Mission Santa Ynez.

The post-World War II boom in travel by car had a major effect on Buellton. Highway 101 was expanded to two lanes in both directions, with two-lane access roads on either side. The town welcomed the enlarging of its meal ticket even though it required the tearing down or moving of many of the town buildings to accommodate the much wider highway. The greater presence of the highway also led to the addition of many new gas stations, restaurants, and motels. So great was the transformation that the California State Highways Department began referring to Buellton as "Service Town USA."

Buellton, "Service Town USA"

Andersen's Electric Café, ca 1925

Hap-pea and Pea-wee welcome you to the new Andersen's, ca 1948

There was always at least one good reason to stop at Buellton even if you did not need gas. Anton Andersen had been a chef at the Biltmore Hotels in New York and Los Angeles. He moved to the new town of Buellton in 1924 and opened Andersen's Electrical Café. The restaurant was an immediate hit but became a sensation after his wife Juliette started offering her French mother's recipe for split pea soup. A larger restaurant and an attendant hotel, named the Bueltmore in reference to Anton's former employer, opened in 1928. Before long signposts appeared on 101 featuring the restaurant's mascots Hap-pea and Pea-wee who urged motorists to stop in for a meal. Andersen's was enlarged when it was moved due to the expansion of 101 in 1948, thriving as both a restaurant and motel. It has survived all of Buellton's changes over its ninety-year existence and remains the town's chief attraction.

EL CAMINO REAL — HIGHWAY 101 & THE ROUTE OF THE *DAYLIGHT*

New Highway 101 freeway moves east of Andersen's, ca 1950

Buellton quickly became a victim of its own success. The traffic at the intersection of 101 and 246 became so congested that the town welcomed the 1965 movement of the highway farther east, completely by passing the town. The multiple lanes of old 101 as they ran through town were turned into the Avenue of Flags and a city park. But Buellton remained the off-ramp for Lompoc, Mission La Purisima, Solvang, and Mission Santa Ynez. Perhaps its greatest attraction is the gateway to the Santa Barbara County wine country. Andersen's continues to pull people off the freeway as do the still plentiful gas stations and motels. As a bedroom community for Santa Barbara and Goleta, thirty miles to the south, Buellton and its surrounding towns, Santa Ynez, Los Olivos, Ballard, and Solvang have become one of the fastest growing areas in Santa Barbara County.

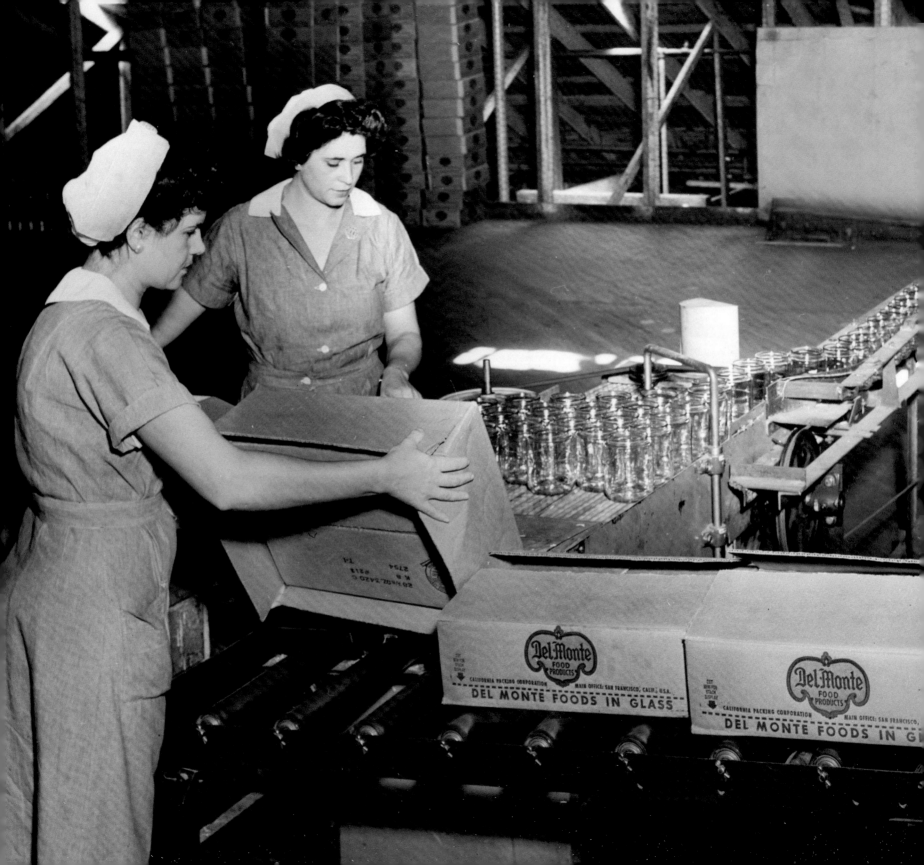

Chapter Five

Two Towns: San Jose and San Luis Obispo

Through the first half of the twentieth century, the Santa Clara Valley was known as "The Valley of Heart's Delight" for its physical beauty and the fragrance of thousands of blooming fruit trees. San Jose was the county seat of that agricultural abundance. Led by Del Monte, it was the canning capital of California.

San Jose started as the first Spanish pueblo in Alta California. Reflecting the nearby Guadalupe River, it was established as San Jose de Guadalupe on November 29, 1777. It was developed as an agricultural pueblo to help feed the presidios of Monterey and San Francisco. The mission called San Jose was actually located 13 miles north in the current city of Fremont on the eastern side of lower San Francisco Bay. Mission Santa Clara de Asis was closer to San Jose, and today the city of Santa Clara is contiguous with the City of San Jose. While San Jose was only briefly the capital of the state (1849-51), it soon became and remained a leading agricultural center. Its status as an agricultural center on the San Francisco Bay led to its connection with San Francisco by stagecoach in 1858 and train in 1864. By World War II San Jose was the world's leading canning and dried fruit packing center with eighteen canneries and thirteen packinghouses.

Tours of the Del Monte factory were a lure for the traffic streaming through San Jose on the pre-World War II Highway 101. But it was the public's fascination with the Winchester House of Mystery that caused tourists to stop. Sarah Winchester, heiress to the Winchester rifle millions, built a 160-room Victorian mansion beginning in 1884 and continuing until her death in 1922. The story is that she was in such despair over the premature deaths of her daughter and husband that she consulted a medium. She was told to sell her

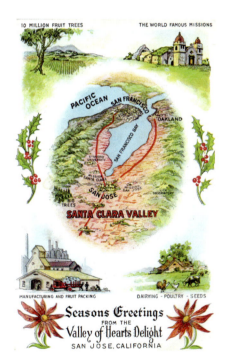

Del Monte "Foods in Glass," San Jose, ca 1940

Glass jar canning, San Jose, ca 1900

United States Products Cannery, San Jose, ca 1942

EL CAMINO REAL — HIGHWAY 101 & THE ROUTE OF THE *DAYLIGHT*

Winchester House of Mystery, San Jose, ca 1950

house in New Haven and move west and build a new house. If she kept building, the spirits of all those killed by Winchester rifles would be stilled and she would keep living. And build she did.

World War II had a lasting impact on the entire state of California. San Jose was no different. While the canning and packing went on to feed a hungry world, manufacturing for the war effort became a major component of the city's economic base.

Key to the city's future, International Business Machines established its West Coast headquarters there in 1943 and opened a research and development office and a manufacturing plant nine years later. San Jose's physical expansion rapidly followed the war, as the city annexed more and more of the surrounding countryside. High tech firms continued to open offices in the Silicon Valley to build on the base established by IBM.

IBM, San Jose Building 25, ca 1956

Workers moving an IBM 305-A RAMAC commercial computer, San Jose, ca 1956

San Jose was aided in this transformation by an excellent system of local universities. Santa Clara was the first university founded in California. It was opened by the Jesuits on the site of the eighth mission in Padre Serra's ladder. Right in town, San Jose State University was the first public university founded in California (1857). Stanford University in nearby Palo Alto came about when one of the Southern Pacific's Big Four, Leland Stanford, went to Harvard University, Charles Eliot, president, and asked how he could create the equivalent of that redoubtable institute in the West.

By the 1990s San Jose was a completely transformed city. Long gone was the agriculturally dominated economy of canning. It had been replaced by cutting-edge technology in electronics and computers. The population graph for San Jose from

Oracle, Redwood Shores, Silicon Valley, 2012

Santa Clara University, ca 1965

San Jose State College (now University) "La Torre", ca 1955

Aerial view of Stanford University, Palo Alto, 2012

Downtown San Jose from Plaza de César Chávez originally the site of California's first state capitol from 1849 to 1851, 2012

1950 to 2010 looks like a rocket launching. During those sixty years, the population rose from 95,280 to 945,942. San Jose, now the third largest city in the state, rightly proclaims itself the "Capital of Silicon Valley," and its state university's motto is "Powering Silicon Valley."

IBM data processing equipment being loaded on a Douglas DC-6A, ca 1958

San Luis Obispo dry farming, ca 1910

Like the far more populous city to the north, San Luis Obispo was an agricultural county seat for most of its existence. It started as an adjunct to the fifth mission in the ladder, named for St. Louis, the Bishop of Toulouse, France, who was a Franciscan priest that renounced an inheritance of secular titles and great wealth to serve the church. The area had two claims to mission history. When the first four missions were on the verge of starvation in 1772, a hunting party was sent to an area recorded as the Plain of the Bears by Gaspar de Portola's diarist, Father Juan Crespi. The meat they gathered was loaded on twenty-five mules and saved the mission system. The church also led the way in roofing the missions with tile. Two thatch roofs were burned off the building by flaming arrows fired by hostile Indians. The padres decided that tile would make better roofing, and it soon became common all through the ladder of missions.

San Luis Obispo settled into its role as the agricultural shipping point for the surrounding farms. It became a major local railroad center due to its position at the base of the Cuesta

Construction of Highway 101 over the Cuesta Grade, ca 1924

Grade. The Chinese laborers who built the lines south to Paso Robles and spent almost a decade digging the tunnels and forming the grades through the Cuesta Grade mostly lived in San Luis Obispo's Chinatown. With the twentieth century and the development of Highway 101 motorists added a new component to San Luis Obispo. Being almost exactly halfway between Los Angeles and San Francisco, the town became a major stopping point. In 1925 brothers Alfred and Arthur Heineman decided to become innkeepers. At this time, travelers had the option of pitching a tent, staying in a primitive auto court, or stopping at a downtown hotel as they traveled along the Coast Highway. The Heineman's thought a good room where you could park your car would be just the ticket for all the new auto travelers. They opened the Milestone Motor Hotel on the northern outskirts of San Luis Obispo at the base of the Cuesta Grade. Known as the Motel Inn, it was an immediate hit with motorists and started a whole new industry. Motels started to spring up all over the country.

Ah Louis store, 800 Palm Street, downtown San Luis Obispo, ca 1943

Motel Inn originally known as Milestone Mo-Tel on Highway 101 at north end of San Luis Obispo, ca 1927

San Luis Obispo was on California's Mission Trail, but it was far from a key stop. Paul Elder expressed the common disappointment of the mission traveler in 1915 when he noted, "The Mission church has been restored, unfortunately without reference to traditions, and being on a prominent street of a busy town, it has lost all of the peculiar Mission individuality. The walls are boarded, the roof shingled; and most deplorable, a tower 'for all the world like an old-fashioned New England meeting-house steeple' has been erected." Hildegarde Hawthorne was equally unimpressed with the whole town. She noted in 1938 that San Luis Obispo is "a small place…You can walk over it in an hour or two."

Besides the motels, what kept pre-World War II San Luis Obispo important to the 101 experience was that it was where State Highway 1 branched off to the northwest, leading to Morro Bay, Cayucos, Cambria, William Randolph Hearst's magnificent castle on the hill above San Simeon, and the gran-

Mission San Luis Obispo in Victorian era prior to restoration, ca 1915

Southwest corner of Morro and Monterey Streets. The Liberty Cafe and St. James Hotel with $1.00 a night lodging and running water were located on Highway 101, as indicated on the lamppost sign.

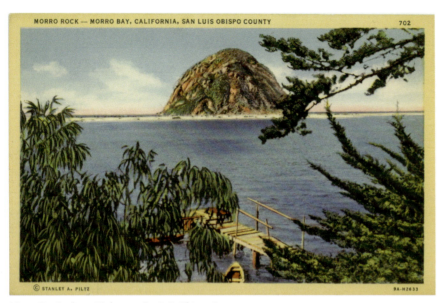
Morro Bay Rock, on Highway 1, San Luis Obispo Country, ca 1940

Welcome to Cayucos on Highway 1, 1973

Hearst Castle, San Simeon on Highway 1, ca 1960

Bixby Creek Bridge on Highway 1, ca 1940

Monterey Marina, ca 1960

deur of Big Sur. Continuing north, Highway 1 passes over one of the most beautiful and functional bridges in the country at Bixby Creek. That part of the highway took eighteen years to build. But in 1937 Monterey and Carmel by the Sea were finally connected to Cambria and San Luis Obispo by a modern, two-lane highway. Like its brother, US 101, Highway 1 is nothing to take if you are in a hurry. But if you want to drive slowly through some of the most spectacular views in the United States, it has to be your choice.

Like everywhere else along the 101, San Luis Obispo was greatly affected by World War II. Camp Merriam, the local California National Guard base, was turned into Camp San Luis Obispo by the U.S. Army between Fall, 1940 and Summer, 1941 and quickly became a major infantry training base. Farther north in Paso Robles, Sherwood Field, a civilian flying field, was taken over by the Army Air Corps for pilot training in 1941 and significantly expanded. Well over 100,000 soldiers passed through the various local bases. When the war was over, returning veterans who had trained locally became a part of the population explosion of San Luis Obispo County.

San Luis Obispo began its gradual transformation into one of the most physically pleasing towns in America in the late 1970s. Ken Schwartz, a professor in the Architecture and Urban Planning Department at Cal Poly who served on the city council and was elected mayor five times, led a group of city officials and businessmen that slowly converted San Luis Obispo from a haphazard agricultural center to the gem it is today. The first project was to turn the parking lot of the Mission into a city park. That was followed by the excellent decision to keep San Luis Obispo Creek a natural stream and create the sort of riverwalk around it that was so key to revitalizing San Antonio, Texas. Soon the creek was lined with places to eat, art galleries, lower entrances to street-level stores, and ample space to walk in a bucolic environment right downtown. Next came an aggressive policy of tree planting and bicycle paths. You can still walk around San Luis Obispo

Camp San Luis Obispo is the original home of the California Army National Guard established in 1928, formerly called Camp Merriam, ca 1943

in a couple of hours, but you won't find a place that more perfectly melds its old and new buildings.

Like San Jose to the north, San Luis Obispo is affiliated with the mission-era roots of Highway 101. Both towns grew into the major shipping centers for the agriculture that surrounded them. San Jose has become one of the major cities in the state and the epicenter of the continuously expanding high-technology industries. Agriculture continues to be San Luis Obispo's economic foundation. It has become a hub in California's wine industry, with grapes being the chief product of the region. They are followed by strawberries, broccoli, and cattle. But like its northern neighbor, technology and specialized manufacturing have become a growing part of San Luis Obispo's economy. It is worth noting, that in Dan Buettner's 2010 book on the best places to live on earth for the National Geographic press called *Thrive*, he chose San Luis Obispo as North America's premier spot.

Highway 1, Big Sur, winding with beautiful scenery, ca 1970

Ah Louis store (gift shop selling mostly housewares), 800 Palm Street in downtown San Luis Obispo, 2012

EL CAMINO REAL — HIGHWAY 101 & THE ROUTE OF THE *DAYLIGHT*

Chapter Six

One Town: Santa Barbara

The best-known product of the New Deal's Federal Writers Project of the Works Progress Administration (WPA) during the Great Depression was the State Guides. But the WPA also produced a series of city guides. The two smallest towns given their own book were Henderson, Kentucky (home of the artist and naturalist, John James Audubon) and Santa Barbara, California.

Santa Barbara traces its founding to Governor Felipe de Neve in 1782. He needed a military presidio on the central California coast between San Diego and Monterey to protect Spain's claims on the underpopulated territory. After much sparring with the civil administration of Alta California, a mission was eventually built near the presidio by Father Fermin de Lausen, who succeeded Father Serra as president of the missions upon Serra's death. Tenth in the ladder, the current church is the fourth built on the site - the first three succumbing to the need for larger structures as the number of neophytes grew and the horrendous earthquake of December 21, 1812. The new, much larger and far more ornate, building came to be called "the Queen of the Missions." It is the only one of the twenty-one missions that has been served by Franciscans from its inception to the present.

Cattle grazing in Santa Barbara County, ca 1900

Coastal route stagecoach, ca 1861

While the church remained under Franciscan control after secularization, all the other lands associated with the mission during the Spanish era were confiscated by the new Mexican government or sold by the padres. It was a familiar story up and down the ladder of the mission chain. Cattle and their hides became the dominant industry in the Santa Barbara area in the Mexican and early American periods until the tragic draught of the mid-1860s destroyed the ranches. The town stumbled along in spite of its connection by stagecoach in 1861 with the main population center in San Francisco. That did little to alleviate the isolation of the central coast. The stage trip was brutal on what passed for the roads of the day.

Santa Barbara finally became a tourist destination largely due to Charles Nordhoff. His *California for Travelers and Settlers* was published in 1873 and was the first book to spread the word to the rest of the country about the glories of southern California's climate. Santa Barbara came in for special praise. He wrote the town "is on many accounts the pleasantest of all the places I have named." Nordhoff explained this was due to its location on the longest southern facing section of the California coast, protected by a high coast range from "the harsh and foggy north and north-west winds, which make the coast north of Point Conception disagreeable." The travelers lured by Nordhoff's glowing description had a place to land via coastal steamer thanks to John Stearns. In 1872, he built a substantial

California, a book for travellers and settlers, Charles Nordoff, 1872

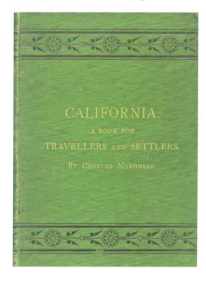

On the beach at beautiful Santa Barbara, ca 1915

Steamer *Santa Rosa* at Santa Barbara wharf, ca 1904

EL CAMINO REAL — HIGHWAY 101 & THE ROUTE OF THE *DAYLIGHT*

The Arlington Hotel, ca 1909

Below: Hotel Potter, ca 1907

wharf on the waterfront at the foot of State Street and it's now known as Stearns Wharf. They had a wonderful place to stay up State Street away from the water when the Arlington was opened as El Camino Real's first great resort hotel on July 10, 1875.

Growth was rapid in Santa Barbara after the railroad connection with Los Angeles was made on August 20, 1887. The main draw continued to be the almost perfect climate to be found in the city. But uncommonly for the era, the mission was also a major attraction. Most of the missions in the ladder were in various states of ruin in the late nineteenth century and had yet to become important tourist stops. Santa Barbara was always unique in that the mission never fell to ruin, it remained in the hands of the Franciscans, and it was by far the most imposing of all the structures left from the Spanish past. So, when Pasadena photographer and bookseller A.C. Vroman produced one of the first guides to California's missions in 1893, Mission Santa Barbara was featured. He noted that it was readily available from Los Angeles by the Southern Pacific Railroad, and unlike most of the other mission sites, there was a direct connection by streetcar just two miles away from the train station.

By the time the Southern Pacific's coastal route was finally completed in 1905, Santa Barbara was well established as a tourist destination. The Potter opened in 1903 as a second resort hotel joining the Arlington. Stearns Wharf was still the port of call for steamships to Santa Barbara. Besides tourism, the surrounding area had become a significant citrus growing area after the turn of the century, and the Flying A Studio moved to Santa Barbara from La Mesa, California, in 1912, making the northern city a rival to Hollywood for movie production. The completion of the coast highway for automobiles by the second decade of the new century further increased the lure of the town due to ease of transportation.

Flying "A" Studios, American Film Manufacturing Company, ca 1915

Santa Barbara became an immediate destination for California's autoists. Thomas Murphy, author of *On Sunset Highways*, arrived by motor car in 1921 to stay at the Arlington. On visiting the mission, he and his wife were given a tour by one of the priests. They noted the tour did not include the padre's walk and garden since the only woman who could enter was the "reigning queen," or in the case of the United States, the first lady. Following their tour of the mission, the couple hired a horse-drawn carriage to see the town and surrounding territory since the local roads were inadequate for motor travel. Murphy loved their stop, observing, "There is no other town of the size in California – or scarcely of any size, for that matter – that has about it such a wonderful series of drives and walks as Santa Barbara."

Bath House and Plaza Del Mar, ca 1908

Four years later, "Mission Play" author John Steven McGroarty produced a pamphlet for the Southern Pacific on Santa Barbara with photographs by Samuel Adelstein. After sketching out the history of the town, McGroarty summed up its unique appeal. "You may have wandered far, seeing much of the world, but you will have seen no sweep of sea and sky, no golden hills or sun-swept mountain slopes quite to rival these that you will feast your soul from the uplifted heights of the Santa Ynez. The European Riviera can not compare with it, the age-old glamour of the Phoenician pathways of the Mediterranean are not so alluring; there is not anywhere else, I am sure, the same indescribable fascination… [It] is really the loveliest spot in all the world."

Katherine Taylor visited Santa Barbara in 1928 for her *Los Angeles Tripbook*. The city had suffered a major earthquake three years before and chose to rebuild with a strict adherence to a Spanish Colonial architectural style. Taylor liked the changes to the city. She urged a side trip by rail or auto to Santa Barbara that not only has "the best preserved" mission in the chain, but has "a distinctly Mediterranean flavor, a seat of Spanish California's serene civilization, adapted to American life."

In 1932 Lanier and Virginia Bartlett published a wildly enthusiastic tour book called *Los Angeles In Seven Days*. Sunday was the day to hit 101 north to Santa Barbara. After stopping at Mission San Fernando, they went to "The Poinsettia City" of Ventura. They continued north over the new concrete cause-

Mar Monte Hotel, Santa Barbara, 1954

way at Rincon to "the little oil town of Summerland, an eyesore on the otherwise beautiful coastline," on to Carpinteria, "where the avocado trees grow so lush and the bougainvillea so bright." Once past Montecito, they entered Santa Barbara. The couple reveled in the classic, Spanish architecture and street names of the town, visited the mission, strolled about in the wonderful waterfront, and enjoyed its excellent shops.

The 1941 *WPA Guide Book* lacked the gushing prose so evident in the Bartletts' tour book, but it was still taken with Santa Barbara, noting, "a beneficent nature made her a gracious place in which to live." After describing the contemporary city and its history, the guide took readers on several of the "drives and walks" that so impressed Thomas Murphy two decades before that describe "not only the history of California, but also the history of Spain, Mexico, America." Back in the town, the writers, of course, included the mission, noting, "Here was the flowering of the great mission system, and here alone the mission endured."

Tourist volume only increased following the 101's postwar improvements. The 1952 *Mission Trails Guide* lauded not only the mission where "the altar light has never been extinguished," but also the "gracious setting, retaining the rich heritage and

Santa Barbara County Court House, ca 1935

flavor of the Days of the Dons." Attractions in the city had certainly multiplied. Besides the always popular waterfront, the Guide recommended a visit to the Botanical Garden, Museum of Natural History, Andree Clark Bird Refuge, and the historic murals in the Court House.

Santa Barbara has been one of the primary resorts in California since the late nineteenth century. Every time a new form of transportation – from stagecoach to train to automobile – was developed, Santa Barbara became one of the first destinations. It has always been a classy town with an assumption of wealth and elegance. It started out right by having the most ornate and imposing mission in the entire ladder and never lost its presence and uniqueness among all the towns on the coastal route. Recent developments like Fess Parker's Double Tree Resort on the waterfront ensures that the legacy of the Arlington and Potter Hotels will continue into the twenty-first century.

Fess Parker's DoubleTree Resort, 2012

EL CAMINO REAL — HIGHWAY 101 & THE ROUTE OF THE *DAYLIGHT*

Chapter Seven

Green Gold

California is the leading agricultural state in the Union and the fifth largest supplier of food and agricultural commodities in the world. Its key farming valleys – Sacramento and San Joaquin that form the Great Central Valley, Imperial, and Salinas – are almost absurdly fertile. The gentle climate and lush soil watered by one of the most extensive irrigation systems in the world ensure multiple crops each year. From the missions to the first nineteenth century promotional publications by the railroads and chambers of commerce, the dominant appeal to immigrate to California was to farmers.

San Luis Obispo County farming, 2012

Cattle and agriculture were the first things that lured the railroads into the land of El Camino Real. The San Fernando Valley in Los Angeles County and the Salinas Valley in Monterey County were major wheat producing areas in the late nineteenth and early twentieth centuries. As transportation and irrigation methods constantly improved, a staggering variety of crops began to be grown in all the different agricultural zones along the 101. The grapes, olives, and wheat pioneered by the mission priests were the first common crops along the highway. The wheat that flourished in the early dry farming period was eventually supplanted by plums, prunes, persimmons, apricots, figs, cherries, berries, apples, peaches, lemons, oranges, walnuts, almonds, avocados, lettuce, beets, tomatoes, and sugar beets when irrigation was implemented. The seaside village of La Conchita in Ventura County even managed to produce bananas, which had always been deemed impossible to grow in California's climate.

Opposite: Threshing operation with 21 posed men, Ovefelt Threshing Machine, San Luis Obispo County, ca 1880

Above, right: A field of calla lilies near Ventura, ca 1908

Padres harvesting hay, Mission Santa Barbara, ca 1905

Following pages: Cornucopia of Coastal California agriculture, Edward H. Mitchell – post cards, ca 1905

EL CAMINO REAL — HIGHWAY 101 & THE ROUTE OF THE *DAYLIGHT*

EL CAMINO REAL — HIGHWAY 101 & THE ROUTE OF THE *DAYLIGHT*

EL CAMINO REAL — HIGHWAY 101 & THE ROUTE OF THE *DAYLIGHT*

CALIFORNIA
AGRICULTURAL AND GRAZING LANDS

ARE OFFERED FOR SALE BY

SOUTHERN PACIFIC COMPANY

IN VARIOUS LOCALITIES THROUGHOUT THE STATE
ADJACENT TO ITS RAILROAD LINES

For information, maps and price lists address Land Department, Southern Pacific Company, 65 Market St., San Francisco, Cal., or 829 Story Bldg., 610 So. Broadway, Los Angeles, Cal.; for specific data concerning railroad or other lands in the particular locality, address any of the following named Sales Agents:

Rounding up the herd, ca 1910

Agriculture was a key aspect of the mission system. The Franciscans introduced the Indians to a European way of life so they could eventually lead independent, productive lives within the Spanish colonial framework. To achieve that end, the neophytes were not only instructed in religious dogma, but were also taught useful skills. Shops were set up to teach the neophytes how to tan and form leather, blacksmithing, weaving, construction work, wine making, candle making, irrigation methods, and every other skill to keep the largely self-sufficient missions in operation. But the primary task was farming and cattle raising. The most successful of the missions in this regard were San Juan Capistrano, San Gabriel, San Fernando, Santa Ynez, La Purisima, San Miguel, and San Jose.

When the Mexicans took over Alta California, the lands of the missions were turned into ranchos. They remained the same under the Americans once California became a state in 1850. Cattle was always a major industry in the state, but it was supplanted by agriculture after the droughts of 1860s caused the death of thousands of animals and the breakup of the large ranchos. This, in turn, led to the gradual populating of the state by Americans in search of prime farm and ranch land.

San Mateo County just south of San Francisco became the home of a multi-million dollar cut flowers industry. Chrysanthemums were the most prolific of the flowers. The Santa Clara Valley just south of all those flowers is one of the most fertile of the smaller valleys in the state. San Jose has always been its commercial capital. Famous now as the heart of Silicon Valley, the city in the early twentieth century was the major canning and shipping center for an agricultural empire. It was still in its earliest agricultural phase when Thomas Murphy toured the area in 1921. He drove the winding road up Mount Hamilton to see the famous Lick Observatory. Once he crested the hill, "Just beneath us lay the wide vale of the Santa Clara – surely one of

Harvesting pears, ca 1905

EL CAMINO REAL — HIGHWAY 101 & THE ROUTE OF THE *DAYLIGHT*

the most beautiful and prosperous of the famous valleys of the Golden State – diversified by orchards and endless wheat fields, with here and there an isolated ranch-house or village."

On the southern end of Santa Clara County, Gilroy is known today as the Garlic Capital of the World due to both the surrounding fields and its packing plants. Their annual Garlic Festival, held the last weekend in July, is one of the great continuing events in California. But Gilroy has been the capital of many agricultural products in its time. It got its start as a stage stop on the San Jose to Monterey Road in 1850. The town was incorporated in 1867, and the railroad arrived two years later. At that time it was on its way to becoming the Tobacco Capital of the United States with one of the world's largest cigar factories. By the late nineteenth century, Swiss immigrants helped

Garlic Festival, Gilroy, 2012

Left: Garlic processing plant, Gilroy, ca 1980

Above: "How about a cigar?" Gilroy-Tobacco Capital of the United States, ca 1910

Opposite: Prune processing, ca 1915

EL CAMINO REAL — HIGHWAY 101 & THE ROUTE OF THE *DAYLIGHT*

EL CAMINO REAL — HIGHWAY 101 & THE ROUTE OF THE *DAYLIGHT*

Celery fields, ca 1908

turn Gilroy into the Dairy and Cheese Capital of California. With the new century and the heavy planting of the French prune, Gilroy became the Prune Capital of California. The town prided itself on making sure every doughboy in France during World War I had all the prunes he could eat. Garlic took over with a rise in Italian and Japanese immigration in the 1930s. It still rules in Gilroy.

But the major topic of any discussion of agriculture along the coastal route is the wildly fertile Salinas Valley farther south in Monterey County. Its most famous son, author John Steinbeck, described the valley of his youth in his 1952 novel *East of Eden*.

"The Salinas Valley… is a long narrow swale between two ranges of mountains and the Salinas River that winds and twists up the center until it falls at last into Monterey Bay… I remember that the Gabilan Mountains to the east of the Valley were light gray mountains full of sun and loveliness

Harvesting in Salinas Valley, ca 1950

and a kind of invitation, so that you wanted to climb into their warm foothills almost as you want to climb into the lap of a beloved mother. They were beckoning mountains with a brown grass love. The Santa Lucia's stood up against the sky to the west and kept the valley from the open sea, and they were dark and brooding – unfriendly and dangerous."

The first important crop produced in the Salinas Valley was wheat. Intrepid autoist Thomas Murphy drove the length of the valley in 1921 on a tour of the missions.

After fording the Salinas River near San Miguel, he happily noted he avoided needing to be dragged out of the riverbed sand by two men with a horse team that were waiting to collect a fee for aiding stuck motorists. Murphy re-crossed the river on the bridge near Bradley, "And for the rest of the day, except when crossing an occasional hill range, we passed through endless wheat fields, stretching away to the distant hills."

The extensive use of irrigation starting in the 1920s transformed the Salinas Valley. It became "America's Salad Bowl." Today, the area's 3.8 billion dollar agricultural industry supplies 80 percent of America's lettuce and nearly as much of

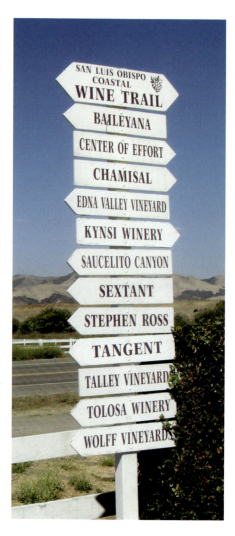

Vineyards near Lompoc, 2012

its artichokes. In Castroville, on the Southern Pacific Coast Line, artichokes were introduced from Italy, Castroville now claims it's "The Artichoke Center of the World." Anything else that might show up in a salad - broccoli, cauliflower, spinach, strawberries, peppers, squash, carrots, asparagus, and celery – are grown in abundance in the Salinas Valley. The most recent crop is grapes for the numerous wineries that have grown up in the area. That incredible bounty has made Salinas and King City into major agricultural shipment centers whose products reach every corner of the United States as well as Canada, Mexico, Japan, Hong Kong, Taiwan, and Europe. The Salinas Valley is also the best of California's major agricultural valleys to traverse in a motorcar. It is just wide enough to provide constantly changing vistas and is always tantalizing to the eye.

The southern counties also play a major role in California's agricultural dominance. San Luis Obispo County is home to a growing wine grape industry, as well as copious amounts of broccoli, strawberries, lettuce, carrots, and cattle. Santa Barbara County plays a large role in the constantly growing California wine industry. All kinds of berries, more lettuce, cauliflower and broccoli, plus lemons, fruits, and nuts represent other common crops throughout the county with the ever-present cattle. The area around Lompoc is a leader in the flower seed industry.

Ventura has been a primary agricultural area since the successful development of Mission San Buenaventura in the early nineteenth century. It was the ninth mission in the ladder and the last founded by Father Serra. One of the reasons the mission proved so fruitful was the seven-mile-long aqueduct built by the neophytes to bring Ventura River water to irrigate the church's land. Livestock raising was the leading commodity of the American period. Beans supplanted this by the turn of the twentieth century.

Ventura Southern Pacific railroad depot, ca 1900

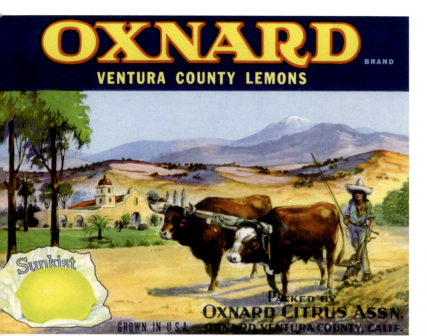

Physical isolation was always a problem with El Camino Real towns. The first effort to improve connection with the rest of southern California was the 1872 pier. It provided wharfage for ships that could now haul off the produce of Ventura's fertile fields. Finally, the railroad arrived to further increase the city and county's availability to markets.

Agriculture thrived in Ventura throughout the twentieth century. Strawberries and citrus supplanted beans. Lemons were particularly successful. The county still accounts for 61 percent of the lemons in California and 47 percent of those in the United States. The lemon crop is so plentiful that Sunkist switched the shipping of lemons from the Port of Long Beach to Port Hueneme in December 1993. Strawberries are the key crop in the county and are clearly visible in the fields and fruit stands along the 101.

Other key crops are celery, avocados, tomatoes, raspberries, peppers, nursery stock, and oranges. But in spite of the continuing success of agricultural production, Ventura County is in a fight to retain its rural character. The population of the county has doubled five times since 1950, and a series of slow-growth laws has been implemented.

A quick look at the crop reports from Santa Clara County show the same phenomena. The city of Salinas continues to grow and diversify, and nearby Spreckels has become a bedroom community with the closing of the huge sugar beet processing plant that gave that town its name. But the Valley of the Salinas River will continue to provide the needs of salad lovers all over the world for the foreseeable future. The padres would be astounded by what has become of the agricultural ventures that started in their missions.

Strawberry fields, Oxnard, 2012

Chapter Eight

Black Gold

Oil was nothing new to the land of the 101. What is known now as the La Brea Tar Pits in mid-Los Angeles was used by the Indians and later the Spanish whenever something needed to be caulked or a roof tarred to keep out the rain. The Santa Barbara County coastal town of Carpinteria (Spanish for carpenter) was named by Don Gaspar de Portola's soldiers who saw Indians making a canoe along the shoreline. The canoes were caulked with the local tar that oozed out of the side of a hill. Farther north in San Luis Obispo County, the "pismo" in Pismo Beach is the Chumash Indian word for "tar," and used by that tribe in the same way as their brothers to the south.

Opposite: Crown Hill, Los Angeles, ca 1900

Until the mid-nineteenth century, all this surface oil was perceived of as being as much a nuisance as a benefit. Oil came from whales, not the ground. It was not until the 1859 discovery of oil in Titusville, Pennsylvania, was mated with new drilling techniques, a railroad to transport it, and the knowledge of how to refine it that oil became a positive commodity. In 1892, oil was first successfully drilled in the Los Angeles area when failed miners Edward Doheny and Charles Canfield sank their first well on Crown Hill using a sharpened eucalyptus tree. Other sites followed all over southern California until by 1923 California was the leading oil producer in the United States and was the source of one-quarter of the world's output of oil.

The state's remoteness to the major population centers of the United States caused local companies to become leaders in the shipping of oil. The Pacific Coast and Union Oil Companies in San Francisco built the S.S. *George Loomis*, the world's first oil tanker. It made its maiden voyage from Ventura in January 1886.

Petroleum production in Ventura County goes back to the beginning of the American period. In 1866 two of railroad tycoon Leland Stanford's brothers began collecting oil from tunnels in Sulphur Mountain north of Ventura. This led many eastern land speculators to buy up plots of former cattle ranches that came up for sale following the draught of the 1860s that devastated ranching all over southern California. In spite of this, drilling in the area was largely unsuccessful until 1919, when the Ventura Field located in the hills north of the city above the 101 started producing. It reached its production peak in the 1950s, but has continued to be a significant oil field.

Oil is also important in Santa Barbara County. Summerland north of Carpinteria was one of the first fields. It received its name from H.L. Williams, who started a spiritualist colony

Crown Hill derricks along Glendale Boulevard with Pacific Electric PCC cars heading toward the Subway Terminal tunnel, ca 1945

EL CAMINO REAL — HIGHWAY 101 & THE ROUTE OF THE *DAYLIGHT*

Oil fields of Santa Maria, ca 1915

Drilling in the bay, Summerland, ca 1910

Oil Wells in the Pacific between Ventura and Santa Barbara, California

in 1888, featuring a full-time séance room. Oil was first drilled two years later, with the field maturing in the 1890s. For the first time in the world, oil wells were drilled off shore in the ocean from fourteen piers. The spiritualist colony did not last, but the oil field flourished. Increased automobile traffic made the closely built derricks into a tourist attraction by 1915. Nearshore production was phased out after 1940, with the wells eventually being moved farther into the Santa Barbara Channel. Driving through the scenic, perfectly landscaped beach town today, you would have no idea that oil wells once dominated the landscape.

Santa Maria is in the northern part of Santa Barbara County and remains its largest town. The fertile soil of its surrounding valley brought in farmers in the early American period. The town was founded in 1875 and prospered as an agricultural center. The new century brought on the expansion of commercial flower-seed growing and oil. The earliest petroleum deposits were first discovered in 1888. It became a significant part of the local economy with the discovery of the enormous Santa Maria Valley Oil Field right under the town in the 1930s. The coming of the 101 brought many more auto-related businesses, but unlike Buellton, Santa Maria never relied on tourists for its economic well-being. Agricultural and petroleum production expanded as the century wore on. They were joined by aerospace concerns with the rapid expansion of the Western Test Range component of Vandenberg Air Force base after 1965.

View of Avila and Port San Luis, Calif.

San Ardo oil fields, 2012

Three pipelines from the Santa Maria fields flow north to Port San Luis, which is also the recipient of oil via pipelines from the vast fields in Kern County. Besides its busy oil port, San Luis Obispo County is known to have petroleum deposits that have yet to be fully exploited. Such is not the case farther north on the 101 at San Ardo in Monterey County at the southern end of the Salinas Valley. The small town was originally planned in 1887 by M.J. Brandenstein when the railroad reached his land. Ranching and agriculture were joined by petroleum when the first wells were drilled by the Texas Company (later Texaco) in 1947. The oil field is south of the small town, while the extremely productive agriculture fields of the Salinas Valley spread north immediately from the town limits. The Evergreen Café that was part of the Shell station on the north end of town and the Traveler's Home Court that was connected to the Union Oil Station in the middle of town survived the end of World War II. They closed following the widening of 101 and the bypassing of San Ardo in the 1970s. The auto court is still there, but is now rented out as small apartments. Nonetheless, San Ardo is very much a functioning town even without the 101 running down its main street or motels to house tourists. Bountiful agriculture and plentiful oil ensure that.

Petroleum production continues to be one of the key components of California's economy in the twenty-first century. The state ranks as the fourth in oil extraction in the Union. While it may not be the first thing people associate with the 101, oil has been a major product along the Coast Route for well over a century and plays a significant role in the close to one million barrels a day that are currently produced by California's wells.

Original Highway 101 near San Ardo, 2012

EL CAMINO REAL — HIGHWAY 101 & THE ROUTE OF THE *DAYLIGHT*

Chapter Nine

The Route of the Military

Like the entire West, California has a long history with the United States military. El Camino Real connected the Spanish presidios during the colonial period and it continued to play a major military role from the dawn of the American period during the Mexican War of 1846-48. The key battles of the conflict were primarily fought on Mexican soil. California was on the periphery of the fighting, but El Camino Real played a part in what fighting there was. On September 26, 1846, Juan Flaco ("Thin John," real name John Brown), began an epic fifty-two hour ride to tell Commodore Robert Stockton in San Francisco that the Los Angeles garrison was about to be overrun by Mexican forces. The warning sent Lt. Col. John C. Fremont marching south to Los Angeles. On his way to attack Santa Barbara he was warned that the city's Mexican garrison had set up an ambush at Gaviota Pass. So the general led his men over the alternative coastal route – San Marcos Pass – only to find the troops had gone to Los Angeles to support Pio Pico's army. Fremont signed the treaty ending the fighting in California at the Campo de Cahuenga in the pass between Los Angeles and the San Fernando Valley on January 13, 1847.

Opposite: Mass at Mission San Antonio de Padua, U.S. Army, 4th Infantry Division, June 1941

San Diego, San Pedro, and San Francisco as California's major port cities had a major military presence since before World War I. Once World War II was on the horizon, California with its mild climate and empty spaces was heavily utilized for the training bases needed to fight a two-front war. Highway 101 was improved as a major roadway for military movement. The Southern Pacific coastal route was alive with troop and freight trains shipping all manner of produce and products to the main ports in Los Angeles and San Francisco as well as supplying the innumerable defense plants up and down the coast and various points in the rest of the nation. Part of the reason the Southern Pacific was so busy was that the role of Los Angeles was dramatically different in the two world wars. In World War I, the city donated great quantities of citrus fruit and oil

Looking north across the Golden Gate from Fort Point, ca 1908

El Presidio de San Francisco was fortified in September 1776 as one of the original Alta California presidios, San Francisco, ca 1908

"Arsenal of Democracy" at work, ca 1943

Left: Lockheed Aircraft Company constructed 9,200 P-38 Lightning planes, Burbank, ca 1943

Above: U.S. Army Recreational Camp, Pismo Beach, 1943

Hangar One, construction covers eight acres, Moffett Field, Mountain View, 1933

and 21,761 of its sons to the various branches of the military to advance the war effort. In World War II, Los Angeles was second only to Detroit as a manufacturing center for the Arsenal of Democracy, namely its aircraft industry.

Military bases were all along Highway 101. An auxiliary lighter-than-air base was established at Lompoc to supplement the key base at Moffett Field in Sunnyvale, which was originally built for the *U.S.S. Macon* dirigible in 1931. The World War II blimps were used to patrol the coast for signs of submarine activity. One of the oddest cases on the home front involved a 101-based blimp. The L-8 based at Moffett Field left Treasure Island in San Francisco Bay on August 16, 1942. After a radio message that they were going to investigate an oil slick, the blimp was not heard from until it crash-landed on a residential street in Daly City. The engines were in perfect running order and the gasbag had not been breached. But there was absolutely no trace of the two-man crew. They had simply disappeared. Seventy years later the case remains a mystery.

The key naval aviation base in California remained the North Island Naval Air Station in San Diego. But Naval Auxiliary Air Stations appeared at Goleta, Monterey, and Point Mugu near Oxnard. Point Mugu was also home to an anti-aircraft gunnery-training center. Port Hueneme in southern Ventura County was only established as a port in 1940. In 1942 it became the West Coast headquarters of the newly inaugurated naval construction battalions, nicknamed the Seabees.

But it was the Army that was most in evidence along the 101 during World War II. Fort Ord at Monterey was established in 1917 and expanded to 2,000 acres and became a major training facility in 1940. The base was named for General Edward Ord, a key leader during the Civil War, who is chiefly remembered for producing the first survey and map of Los Angeles in 1849.

USS *Macon* (ZRS-5), Moffett Field, crashed in a storm off Point Sur, 1933

Douglas B-18, manufactured by Douglas Aircraft Company, Moffett Field, ca 1940

EL CAMINO REAL — HIGHWAY 101 & THE ROUTE OF THE *DAYLIGHT*

Harbor at Port Hueneme Naval Base, Ventura County, home of the Self Defense Test Ship operated by Port Hueneme Division Naval Surface Warfare Center, and three visiting Navy ships from San Diego, February 2010

Fort Hunter Liggett, named for Lieutenant General Hunter Liggett who served from the Indian Wars through World War I, was another massive training facility opened west of King City in 1940. It was created out of 2,000 acres of land purchased from William Randolph Hearst that included not only what his architect Julia Morgan designed as "Hacienda," but also the ruins of Mission San Antonio de Padua. The varied terrain made it a perfect training base for the large field maneuvers, including live fire exercises mainly preparing the recruits for overseas duty. Fort Hunter Liggett was strictly a training facility with no headquarters or command unit on site. It was controlled by Camp Roberts and therefore not publicized by post cards or memorabilia.

Farther south along the 101, Camp Cooke was created out of 86,000 acres of ranch land between Lompoc and Santa Maria. Included in the base was the former Marshallia Dude Ranch. It was named for General Philip Cooke. While a colonel during the Mexican War, he led a battalion from Missouri to California, opening the first wagon route to California. Both armored and infantry troops trained at the enormous base. Like most of the 101 bases, Camp Cooke was once again a hive of activity as a training facility for the Korean War. It was deac-

Armed Services Day parade in front of Mission San Luis Obispo, 1943

tivated in 1953. Four years later the Air Force moved in and the name was changed to Vandenberg Air Force Base. It eventually became the predominant West Coast ballistic missile base and a key component in the American exploration of space.

The 44,000-acre training facility, Camp Roberts north of Bradley was opened in 1940 and named for World War I Medal of Honor winner Corporal Harold Roberts, who was born in San Francisco. Camp Roberts has been a major California National Guard training base since the Army left in 1971.

The original home of the California National Guard was south on the 101 at Camp Merriam, established in 1928. In 1940 the name was changed to Camp San Luis Obispo when it was

EL CAMINO REAL — HIGHWAY 101 & THE ROUTE OF THE *DAYLIGHT*

Camp San Luis Obispo, ca 1942

acquired by the Army and expanded from 6,000 to 15,000 acres on the plains and hills between San Luis Obispo and Morro Bay off Highway 1. It became an infantry training base supplying troops for both the Pacific and European theaters of war. The camp reverted to guard control in 1946, only to be activated by the Army again to train infantry for the Korean War. Since 1965 it has remained under the control of the California National Guard.

Highway 101 was in sight of one of the few direct attacks on the United States during World War II. The first shelling of mainland America since the War of 1812 occurred at the Ellwood Oil Field near Goleta on the evening of February 23, 1942. The Japanese submarine *I-17* surfaced off the beach and began firing at the Richfield aviation fuel tank at Elwood. They missed the tank but destroyed a derrick and pump house and caused some damage to the pier by colliding with it. Jitters from this actual attack could have played a part in the "Battle of Los Angeles," which occurred the next night. Anti-aircraft guns all around the city fired over 1,400 shells in an hour-long barrage. It never has been ascertained what exactly everyone was shooting at.

Endangered merchant ships were also a fact of life off the 101 in the last two weeks of December 1941. The *S.S. Montebello* left Port San Luis near Avila Beach on December 23 and was sunk by a torpedo from Japanese submarine *I-21*. All 36 crewmen got into lifeboats, some of which were fired at by the submarine. All survived and beached near Cambria. The *S.S. H.M. Storey* was luckier the day before. The *I-19* fired three torpedoes at her off Point Arguello north of Santa Barbara and missed.

On Christmas day the *S.S. Absuroka* was hit by the same sub off Point Fermin after leaving San Pedro. It was towed and beached at Fort MacArthur just above San Pedro.

Wartime service continues to be celebrated along the 101. It is signed as part of the Purple Heart Trail that so far

Loading military trucks, ca 1942

runs through twenty states honoring those military men and women wounded or killed while fighting in the defense of the United States. The signs now run from Buellton in Santa Barbara County to San Ardo in Monterey County. Up north at Redwood City, 101 becomes the Military Service Women's Memorial Highway. At San Mateo it becomes Civilian Women Volunteers of All Wars Memorial Highway. It is fitting that the 101 is home to these honors for American veterans. That highway, and the railroad served a major role in both the Arsenal of Democracy and the training of troops in World War II and the Korean Conflict. It is a unique part of the highway's historic legacy.

EL CAMINO REAL — HIGHWAY 101 & THE ROUTE OF THE *DAYLIGHT*

Chapter Ten

A Place to Stop

Opposite: Boeing 314 Clipper, Golden Gate International Exposition, 1939

Below: Powell and Market Streets showing turntable, San Francisco, ca 1940

San Francisco and Los Angeles were both high on the list of stops for anyone vacationing in the far western United States. But both were major cities where open land was at a premium. San Francisco had its luxury hotels, the St. Francis on Union Square being the most prominent. Los Angeles always had its first-class hotels. Going from the Pico House, the Van Nuys to the Alexandria and finally the Biltmore downtown, each hotel was larger and more elegant than the last. The Ambassador in the largely undeveloped western reaches of Los Angeles was as close to being a resort hotel as was possible in city limits.

Space was not such a limitation along the former El Camino Real. Small towns offered both cheap land and a need to make people stop. Huge resort hotels with lots of room and very attentive staffs began to appear. The first was the magnificent Hotel del Monte in Monterey. It was the brainchild of Charles Crocker and was designed by Southern Pacific architect Arthur Brown, and largely constructed by Southern Pacific workers. Derided as "Crocker's Folly," the hotel opened in 1880 and was an immediate success. It burned down in 1887, was rebuilt and opened by the next year only to burn down again in 1924. Both of the early incarnations were wooden Gothic structures. The final building was in the Spanish Revival style, built of reinforced concrete.

Above: Biltmore Hotel, Los Angeles, ca 1923

Right: Ambassador Hotel, Los Angeles, ca 1938

Hotel del Monte, Monterey, ca 1908

By this time the hotel had acquired thousands of additional acres to construct the Pebble Beach golf course, auto and horse tracks, tennis courts, swimming pools, and facilities for deep-sea fishing. Crocker had also established the original Seventeen Mile Drive through the historic and scenic points in Monterey and Pacific Grove. Like so many other of California's older luxury resorts, the Hotel del Monte was taken over by the military during the war. It became a naval pre-flight school in 1943, was purchased outright by the Navy in 1947, and became part of its Naval Post-Graduate School in 1951.

Paso Robles is about halfway between Los Angeles and San Francisco. Its hot springs had been popular with the Salinan Indians living in the area long before the establishment of El Camino Real. The founding of Mission San Miguel ten miles north did not diminish the popularity of the springs. The mission's pastor, Father Juan Cabot, had rheumatism and was a frequent visitor to the hot springs. He built the first structure over them and continued to share the waters with Indian converts. The first hotel to take advantage of the waters was

Left: Seventeen Mile Drive, Monterey

Right: Paso Robles Hot Springs Hotel, ca 1923

Jesse James (about 18 years old) at the time of his visit to Paso Robles, 1865

a small affair of fourteen rooms. Called the Hot Springs Hotel, it opened on what was then called Stagecoach Road in 1864. One of its developers was Drury James, key founder of the town of Paso Robles. His nephews, the outlaws Frank and Jesse James, stayed with him in 1868. Jesse often used the hot springs during his stay to help heal from two gunshot wounds he received in one of the pair's bank robberies.

The small hotel was replaced in 1891 by the grand El Paso de Robles Hotel and became a destination point for eastern travelers and, eventually, California's new autoists. One of its key guests was the virtuoso pianist and eventual Prime Minister of the Republic of Poland, Ignacy Jan Paderewski. He had been experiencing problems with his hands for years. In 1913 his friend Sir Henry Heymann suggested he try the hot springs and mud baths of Paso Robles. He stayed at the hotel for three weeks. So impressed was he at the result, Paderewski purchased land in the area. Sadly, the El Paso de Robles suffered the fate of so many of the huge resort hotels of its era and burned to the ground December 12, 1940. It was rebuilt as a central hotel building with several outlying structures in its original spot on Spring Street, which was Highway 101 before the bypass. It was a mainstay of soldiers at nearby Camp Roberts during World War II and is still going strong.

The Santa Maria Inn was opened in that Santa Barbara County community in 1917. It did not have the scenic grandeur of the Hotel del Monte or the hot springs of Paso Robles, but it was nonetheless the kind of sprawling, generously landscaped resort hotel beloved of California tourists. It is also still in business, serving the burgeoning agricultural, petroleum, and aerospace center that Santa Maria has become. Parts of the original inn are incorporated into the contemporary building. The restaurant, in particular, leads you right back into the era of elegance that was so much a part of El Camino Real's resort hotels.

San Luis Obispo had its own grand hotel in the Hotel Ramona. It opened in 1889 and soon became the social center

EL CAMINO REAL — HIGHWAY 101 & THE ROUTE OF THE *DAYLIGHT*

Hotel Ramona, San Luis Obispo, ca 1889

of the town. It did not have the extensive grounds of the Hotel del Monte but did have croquet fields and offered buggy rides down to Avila Beach and Avila Hot Sulphur Springs. Like so many of its brothers, the Hotel Ramona was the victim of fire in 1906. The unique Madonna Inn is the largest hotel in the San Luis Obispo area today. The original motel on the grounds was built in 1958 with the inn portion added on in 1960. It was rebuilt in 1966 after another fire. Guests can now choose from among the Caveman, Safari, Bridal Falls, or dozens of other themed rooms. Besides the excellent dining room and bakery, another attraction is the hand-carved marble balustrade in the Gold Rush dining room that came from Hearst Castle.

The major resort hotels all featured fine restaurants. But they were not the only places to eat along the 101. Ever since

Madonna Inn, San Luis Obispo, ca 1969

Madonna Inn, Safari guest room, San Luis Obispo, ca 1969

Radio Center, Sunset Boulevard near Vine Street, Hollywood, ca 1935

NBC Studio, Sunset Boulevard at Vine Street, Hollywood, ca 1935

Earl Carroll Theatre, Sunset Boulevard, Hollywood, ca 1938

Musso & Frank Grill, Hollywood Boulevard, 2012

1920 food has been served at the old hotel building in Casmalia off Highway 1 in Santa Barbara County. The Ostini family has been running the restaurant as The Hitching Post ever since 1952. It is one of the best places in California to eat for those who fancy their steaks, chicken. or fish barbequed with red oak wood. The original restaurant was doing so well that a second Hitching Post was opened in Buellton in 1986. It was featured in *Sideways*, the 2004 movie that followed the adventures of two friends in the Santa Barbara County wine country.

One of Los Angeles' most venerable bar and restaurants just missed being on 101. Musso and Frank's has been serving up reliable food since before most of Hollywood's streets were paved. The original plan for the 1934 realignment of 101 called for the route to follow Hollywood Boulevard from its intersection with Vermont Avenue. At that time, Hollywood Boulevard had made itself into one of the premier shopping districts in Los Angeles and merchants did not want to have passerby traffic clogging their street. So Sunset Boulevard was chosen. The 101 passed by the splendid Earl Carroll Theater and NBC and CBS's radio studios instead.

Joe's Cafe has been serving steak dinners on Santa Barbara's State Street since 1923. In 2007 new owner Gene Montesano

Joe's Café, State Street, Santa Barbara, 2012

The Hitching Post Bar-B-Q Steak Restaurant in Casmalia was purchased in 1952 by the Ostini family, 2011

Original Joe's Restaurant, San Jose, 2012

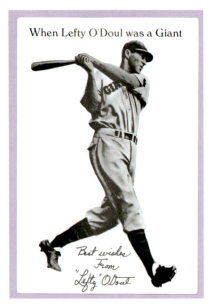
Lefty O'Doul's Restaurant & Cocktail Lounge, San Francisco, ca 1958

Wing's Chinese Restaurant, San Jose, 2012

The Arlington Movie Theater, Santa Barbara, 2012

The Fox Theater, Salinas, 2012

returned Joe's to its 1930s glory. For almost a century the classic all-American hamburger has been the chief product at The Spot a few blocks up from the World's Safest Beach at Carpinteria in Santa Barbara County. It first started feeding hungry beachgoers in 1914.

Farther north along the 101, Rosita's Armory Cafe opened in 1970, making it the oldest continuing Mexican restaurant in Salinas. It is two blocks from Main Street in the refurbished downtown area of Salinas. For those who prefer Chinese food, Wing's has been in business in downtown San Jose on Jackson Street since 1925. Traditional Italian and American meals have been enjoyed at Original Joe's on First Street, also in San Jose, beginning in 1956. At the end of the Bay in San Francisco on Geary Street near Union Square, Lefty O'Doul's has been serving American food in an ambience of Bay Area and national baseball memorabilia since the Giants arrived in 1958. Lefty played with the New York Yankees and several other clubs and eventually became manager of the Pacific Coast League San Francisco Seals. The bar and grill are filled with his memorabilia.

Besides eating and drinking, many 101 towns offered local attractions. Movie attendance was often a bi-weekly experi-

"The World's Safest Beach," mural, Carpinteria, 2012

The Union Hotel, Los Alamos, 2012

ence for many Americans prior to the television revolution of the 1950s. Most of the towns along the 101 had some sort of movie theater, and several had true palaces. The Arlington in Santa Barbara is the best example. It was built on the site of the Arlington Hotel, which was destroyed in the 1925 earthquake. The movie theater was built to make the audience feel it is sitting in a Spanish courtyard with blinking stars in the ceiling. The Majestic Ventura Theater off Main Street in Ventura and the Fox Theater on Main Street in Salinas are both palaces that are part of downtown district that have been refurbished and brought back to life.

The Chamber of Commerce of Carpinteria in Santa Barbara County dreamed up the designation "The World's Safest Beach" to describe their seafront. It was not a total fabrication. The nature of the coast in the area is such that the town's beach presents shallow water for some distance, and beach rescues are virtually unknown.

Los Alamos in Santa Barbara County north of Buellton was bypassed twice. First, by the Southern Pacific Railroad that stayed along the coast and then by the 101 in the 1960s. By the 1980s the town was deep in the economic doldrums. A decision was made to capitalize on the marked antique nature of the town as it existed. The only remaining depot of the narrow-gauge Pacific Coast Railway became the Depot Mall and Pub where antique vendors vie with wine tasting. The Union Hotel was originally a stagecoach stop in the 1880s. It has been fully restored with well-appointed rooms and a magnificent Sunday brunch. The Victorian Mansion dates from 1864 and was moved into town in 1980. It has six themed suites, hidden bathrooms, spiral staircases, and a 1956 Cadillac in the 1950s-themed room. Los Alamos is the beneficiary of the exploding Santa Barbara County wine industry and the nearby Cat Canyon and Orcutt Oil Fields.

"Be sure to return them!" Pismo Beach, ca 1970

Farther north in San Luis Obispo County where the 101 once again meets the coast is the small town of Pismo Beach. Earlier in the twentieth century, it had been the proverbial wide-open town with gambling, and gallons of bootleg liquor. That changed during the Great Depression. Pismo Beach became a resort for tourists largely arriving in the family auto. Besides a pristine beach, the big attraction was the Pismo clam. The town became so famous for its clams that they starred in a Bugs Bunny cartoon. Bugs and Daffy Duck were on their way to Pismo when they took a wrong turn at Albuquerque and wound up in the Arabian Nights. Daffy becomes obsessed with the fortune a genii makes available to him. Bugs has had enough and starts digging his way back to Pismo Beach and those stupendous clams.

Highway 1 is the seaside companion of coastal 101. It breaks off from the 101 at San Luis Obispo and runs to the sea at Morro Bay. Continuing up the coastline, the twisting two-lane highway passes William Randolph Hearst's Castle at San Simeon and continues on to Big Sur, finally reaching Monterey. Big Sur is one of the most spectacular alignments of sea and land in the world. Thousand-foot cliffs running down to the rocky beaches with the Pacific Ocean endlessly pounding on

The 1864 Victorian Mansion, Los Alamos, 2012

EL CAMINO REAL — HIGHWAY 101 & THE ROUTE OF THE *DAYLIGHT*

them. Its wild nature has been the muse to poets Robinson Jeffers, Lawrence Ferlinghetti, and Lillian Bos Ross; novelists Jack Kerouac, Henry Miller, and John Steinbeck; and photographers Edward Weston and Ansel Adams.

In the south, 101 Alternate goes through Malibu. Home to movie stars at the Malibu Colony, during the 1930s it was the site of the Malibu Potteries and its Adamson House headquarters and Thelma Todd's Roadhouse in the Castellammare section of the Pacific Palisades. The Bernheimer Gardens on the bluff above Chautauqua Boulevard was a major tourist attraction prior to World War II. Its reputation suffered during the war because it was owned by Adolph Bernheimer, a German national, and celebrated Japanese art and culture. The gardens did not survive the war, and what was left was sold at auction in 1951.

Two other excellent reasons to use the Coast Road or railroad to get to San Francisco were the international attractions of the 1915 Panama-Pacific International Exposition to cele-

Above: "Pizmo" Beach Hotel, ca 1915

Opposite: Pacific Coast Highway along Malibu at Castellammare, ca 1940

EL CAMINO REAL — HIGHWAY 101 & THE ROUTE OF THE *DAYLIGHT*

Panama-Pacific International Exposition, San Francisco, 1915

brate the opening of the Panama Canal and the 1939-40 Golden Gate International Exposition on Treasure Island – an exposition held on the cusp of the second time the world evolved into a global conflict. The Panama-Pacific Expo predated the automobile revolution. Most of the visitors arrived by train, ship, or ferry boat. The 1939 World's Expo was another story. It was a celebration of the spanning bridges in San Francisco, and many visitors drove their cars over the new Bay Bridge to Treasure Island. Like its New York counterpart, the World of Tomorrow, the Golden Gate International Exposition ran from 1939 to 1940. Within two years, Treasure Island had become a naval base, home to the Navy's Pacific Command war room and a fleet of naval flying boats and blimps.

Treasure Island was decommissioned as a naval base in 1996 and is in the process of becoming a housing development with a spectacular view of San Francisco. The Administration Building of the 1939 Fair is still in use and has a wonderful series of murals on the history of the island.

Today, the melding of past and present is typical of many of the things travelers will find along the 101. A perfect example of a historical reality is Mission La Purisima Concepcion. It was first built in 1787, was a complete ruin in 1900, and today is now a beautifully restored and an excellent reason to get off the highway and visit the mission and the bustling town of Lompoc just west of the mission. Amtrak's *Coast Starlight* passenger train follows the same coast-hugging route through nineteenth and early twentieth century tunnels and trestle bridges as its Depression-era streamlined predecessor. These experiences can be found all up and down the Coast Highway. It offers so many places to stop and learn or to just stop and enjoy. What a more perfect way to see and understand the Golden State that began with just a footpath for the padres.

Golden Gate International Exposition, Treasure Island, San Francisco, 1939-40

Epilogue

Edwin Corle's *The Royal Highway* is a history of El Camino Real published in 1949. The final chapter sums up the highway as it was at mid-century and looked to its future.

> *Today… along former El Camino Real, widening, bridging, streamlining, multiple-laning, bypassing, overpassing and underpassing are still going on. What the highway will look like in 1999 can be pretty well forseen. All major cities will be by-passed, or there will be some form of freeway, the four, six, or even eight main lanes will be graded for speeds of slow-moving vehicles as well as vehicles moving at seventy miles or more an hour, and it should be possible to drive from San Diego to San Francisco in eight to ten hours without breaking either the law or your neck."*

Corle's vision has come true, with not only the large cities bypassed by the highway but the small towns as well. Highway 101 is a modern, high-speed highway tying San Francisco and Los Angeles together. But it is still loyal to its historic routes. Major downtowns in Ventura, Santa Barbara, King City, and Salinas are immediately adjacent to the 101, as are small towns like Carpinteria, Los Alamos, and Soledad. All of the 18th and 19th century Spanish missions, presidios, and pueblos between the two cities remain an integral part of 101 and are readily accessible by off-ramp. The magnificent streamlined Southern Pacific *Coast Daylight* may be only a memory, but Amtrak's *Coast Starlight* travels the same Pacific Ocean, hugging the route of its predecessor while continuing north to Seattle. Fortunately, an original Southern Pacific *Daylight* locomotive (No. 4449) has been restored and is operational. *Daylight* passenger cars have also been preserved to make up the train. It's a must see! Sooner or later, if there are tracks near you, the 4449 will come visiting. Don't miss it.

There is far more to the modern Highway 101 than the chance to visit California's early history. The wine country that used to be associated largely with such northern counties as Napa and Sonoma has spread south. Today, both San Luis Obispo and Santa Barbara Counties are major wine-producing areas. There is an annual Zinfandel Festival in Paso Robles in March, and the Santa Barbara County Vintners Festival takes place in April. The San Luis Obispo vintners hold their annual Harvest Celebration in November. Wine tasting takes place at local vineyards all over the two counties throughout the year. [The 2004 movie *Sideways*

Once upon a time, it was the *Daylight* speeding across the Gaviota trestle; today, it is the Amtrak *Coast Starlight*, December 2011

that concerned the trip taken by a wine connoisseur and his about to be married friend was filmed in Santa Barbara County. The home base of the two was a motel in Buellton.]

Sports of all sorts are at home on the modern 101. The California Rodeo at Salinas is the state's biggest, longest lasting rodeo. It goes back to a Wild West show first held in 1911, which is reminiscent of the festivals held by the Spanish and Mexican rancheros of the 18th and 19th centuries. The modern rodeo held in July is one of the major stops on the Professional Rodeo Cowboys Association circuit and features all the circuit's leading riders, wranglers, and ropers as well as major country music acts. College football will bring 50,000 fans to Stanford Stadium in Palo Alto and 30,000 to San Jose State University's Spartan Stadium. New sports are also celebrated. The annual Kite Expo at Pismo Beach in April is the largest kiteboarding event in the country.

By train or automobile, Highway 101 remains the most historic and physically beautiful transportation corridor in California. The variegated terrain of rolling hills, steep arroyos, soaring trestle bridges, pounding surf, small working towns, resorts, and prosperous cities that mark the coastal route ensures that it will always be a slower way to get from San Francisco to Los Angeles. But it is well worth the extra time. Whether to visit the Franciscan missions, the World's Safest Beach at Carpinteria, the wineries of Santa Barbara and San Luis Obispo, the clams at Pismo Beach, the refurbished Main Streets of Ventura and Salinas or the explosion in size of San Jose, Highway 101 offers a variety of sites for any taste. It is the perfect complement of history, physical beauty, and modern comfort.

With a nose like that it could win the "most handsome" prize at any contest! Photographed at the Los Angeles Union Station, 1989

Bibliography

Bartlett, Lanier, and Virginia Stivers Bartlett. *Los Angeles in Seven Days.* New York: Robert M. McBride, 1932.

Bowler, Ann Martin. *The History of the Paso Robles Inn: More Than a Century of Pride.* Loomis: Oak Lake Press, 2003.

Corle, Edwin. *The Royal Highway: El Camino Real.* New York: Bobbs-Merrill, 1949.

Cragg, Curt. *Images of America: Buellton.* Charleston: Arcadia Publishing, 2006.

Chittenden, Newton. *Health and Pleasure Resorts of the Pacific Coast.* San Francisco: Murdock & Co., 1884.

Elder, Paul. *The Old Spanish Missions of California: An Historical and Descriptive Sketch.* San Francisco: Paul Elder & Co., 1913.

James, George Wharton. *In and Out of the Old Missions of California.* Boston: Little, Brown and Company, 1906.

_____. *Through Ramona's Country.* Boston: Little, Brown and Company, 1909.

Kropp, Phoebe. *California Vieja: Culture and Memory in a Modern American Place.* Berkeley: University of California Press, 2006.

Kurillo, Max, and Erline Tuttle. *California's El Camino Real and its Historic Bells.* San Diego: Sunbelt, 2000.

McGroarty, John Steven. *Mission Memories.* Los Angeles: Neuner Corp., 1929.

Nordhoff, Charles. *California: A Book for Travellers and Settlers.* New York: Harper & Brothers, 1873.

Nordstrom, Alma Algot. *Pen Pictures of California's Missions.* Privately Printed, 1937.

Signor, John R. *Southern Pacific's Coast Line.* Wilton: Signature Press, 1994.

Raycraft, Susan, and Ann Keenan Beckett. *Images of America: San Antonio Valley.* Charleston: Arcadia Publishing, 2006.

Riesenberg, Felix, Jr., *The Golden Road: The Story of California's Spanish Mission Trail.* New York: McGraw-Hill, 1962.

Ryan, Dennis, and Joseph Shine. *Southern Pacific Passenger Trains Volume 2 – Day Trains of the Coast Line.* La Mirada, California: Four Ways West Publications, 2000.

Southern California Writers' Project of the Work Projects Administration. *California: A Guide to the Golden State.* New York: Hastings House, 1939, 1973.

_____. *Los Angeles: A Guide to the City and its Environs.* New York: Hastings House, 1941.

_____. *Monterey Peninsula.* Palo Alto: Stanford University, 1946.

_____. *San Francisco: The Bay and its Cities.* New York: Hastings House, 1941, 1947.

_____. *Santa Barbara: A Guide to the Channel City and its Environs.* New York: Hastings House, 1941.

Tingle, Minnie. *California Missions and Mission Sites Along the King's Highway in 1924.* Los Angeles: T.R. Tingle, 1926.

Tucker, Clifford. *Paso Robles, California, 1930-1950: When Highway 101 Ran Through My Hometown.* Fairfax: History For All, 2009.

Van Dyke, Theodore. *Southern California: Its Valleys, Hills, and Streams.* New York: Fords, Howard & Hulbert, 1886.

Vroman, A. C. *Mission Memories: The Franciscan Missions of California.* Los Angeles: Kinsley-Barnes & Neuner, 1893.

Weber, Msgr. Francis. *The California Missions.* Strasbourg, France: Editions du Signe, 2005.

Wright, Richard K. *Volume 1 Southern Pacific Daylight, Train 98-99.* Thousand Oaks, California: Wright Enterprises, 1970.

Index

Bold Face indicates illustrations

A
Agriculture: 97, 98, 113, 117, 119, 125, 134, 141, **144**, **152-164**, **166**, **167**, 173, 175 Harvesting, **92**, **134**
    Sunkist, 166, Oranges **55**
Alta California: 13, 17, 25, 26, 37, 39, 43, 44, 59, 125, 143, 159, Presidio, **178**
American, 15, 19, 53, 85, 144, 149, 165, 170, 173, 177, 183, 185, 193
Andersen Pea Soup, **112**, 113, **122**, **123**
Authors:
    Bartlett, Lanier & Virginia, 149, 150
    Corle, Edwin, 201
    Hawthorne, Hildegarde, 137
    Jackson, Helen Hunt, 15, 40
    James, George W., 43, 60
    McGroarty, John Steven, 44, 117, 149
    Murphy, Thomas, 17, 148, 150, 159, 163
    Nordhoff, Charles, 45, 144, **145**
    Steinbeck, John, 162, 196
Automobile Club of Southern California, 48, **53**, **57**, 61
Avila Beach, **173**, 184, 190

B
Baja California, 13, 25, 43
Bancroft, A.L. and Company, 21
Bay Bridge, 66, 198
Bayshore Cutoff, 66, 94, **96**
Bernheimer Gardens, 196
Betteravia, 98
Big Sur, 17, 139, **141**, 195
Boosters, 38, 39, 40, **42-44**, 45, 60, 73, 74
Bradley, **113**, **114**, 115, 163, 183
Buellton: 17, 58, 113, **119**, **121**, 122, 123, 173, 185, 191, 194, 200, 201, Nojoqui Grade, 58
Burlingame, 55, 74

C
Cahuenga Pass, **66**
Calabasas, 63
California: 13, 15, 16, 17, 25, 37- 45, 48, 51, 53, 54, 55, 58-61, 63, 73, 74, 85, 87, 92, 93, 100, 125, 128, 130, 141, 143, 147-150, 153, 159, 160, 164, 166, 169, 170, 175, 177, 178, 181, 182, 188, 189, 191, 198, 201, 202
    Tourist Map 1936, **22**, **23**
California Bell Factory, **62**, 63
California Federation of Women's Clubs, 60
California for Travelers and Settlers, 144
California Historic Landmarks League, 38
California Mission Trails, 113
California National Guard, 139, 183, 184
California State Highways Department, 51, 54, 55, 71, 121
California's Mission Trail, 117, 137
Cambria, 137, 139, 184
Carmel by the Sea, **139**
Carpinteria, 150, 169, 170, 193, **194**, 201
Casitas Pass, **53**
Catholic, 15, 37, 38, 115, 130
Chinese, 135, **136**, **141**, 193
Civilian Conservation Corps, 38
Coast Highway, 13, **15**, 16, 19, 45, 51, 53, 55, **58**, 60, **61**, **64**, 65, **70**, 85, 100, 108, 109, 119, 135, 147, 151, 162, 175, 177, 178, 198, 202
Cuesta Grade, **58**, **59**, **65**, **70**, **94**, **135**

D
Daly City, 181
"Days of the Dons", 15, 44, 151
Del Monte Canning, **124**, 125

E
El Camino Real: 1, 13, 16, 25, 26, 31, 38, 39, 41, 43, 44, 45, **46**, 47, 48, 51, **53**, 55, 60, 61, **62**, 63, **68**, 74, 85, 153, 166, 177, 187, 188, 189, 201
    Bell, **48**, **49**, **53**, **57**, **61-63**, 68
El Pasear, **50**, **72-83**

E (cont.)
Elder, Paul, 137
Europe, 19, 26, 164, 149, 159, 184

F
Flaco, Juan, 177
Forbes, Harrie (Mrs. A.S.C.), 45, 47, 48, 60, 61, **62**, 63
Franciscans: 13, 16, 25, 26, **27**, **32**, **39**, 41, 51, 60, 134, **143**, 144, **147**, **159**, 202
    Cabot, Father Juan, 188
    Crespi, Father Juan, 25, 134
    Duran, Father Narciso, 37
    Lausen, Father Fermin de,143
    Moreno, Francisco Garcia Diego y, 37
    "Route of the Padres", 85
    St. Francis Cord, **37**
    Serra, Father Junipero, **2**, 13, **25**, **26**, **143**, **165**
Fremont, 33, 125
Fremont, Lt. Col. John C., 177

G
Gaviota Pass, 58, 70, **71**, 119, 177
Gaviota Trestle, **84**, **85**, 200
Gilroy, **68**, **160**, **161**, 162
Glendale, 108
Golden Gate, 25, **178**, 196
Golden Gate International Exposition, 181, **186**, 196, 198, **199**
Goleta, 123, 181, 184
Great Depression, 13, 100, 143, 195
Guadalupe River, 125

H
Hearst, William Randolph, 137, 182, 195
Heineman, Alfred & Arthur, 135
Highways:
    Lincoln Highway, 59
    Memorial Highway, 185
    Highway 1: 17, 137, **138**, 139, **141**, 184, 191, 195
    Highway 99: 17

Highway 101: 13, **15**, 16, 17, 19, 30, 31, 38, 39, 48, 51, 59, 65, 66, 68, **69**, 70, 113, 115, 117, 119, 121, 122, 123, 125, **135**, 137, 139, 141, 149, 150, 153, 166, 169, 170, 173, **175**, 178, 181, 182, 183, 184, 185, 189, 190, 191, 193, 194, 195, 196, 198, 201, 202
Highway 246: 119, 123
Route 2: 55, 57, 58, 59, 60, 71, 72, 74
Hollywood, 66, 147, **191**
Hotels & Motels: **149**, 187, **188**, 194, 195, 196
    Arlington, 146, 147, 148, 151
    Biltmore, 122, 187, **188**
    El Paso de Robles Hotel, 189
    Fess Parker's Double Tree Resort, **151**
    Hot Springs Hotel, **189**
    Hotel del Monte, 187, **188**, 189, 190
    Hotel Ramona, 189, **190**
    Milestone Motor Hotel (Motel Inn), 135, **136**
    Madonna Inn, **190**
    Potter Hotel, **79**, **146**, 147, 151
    Santa Maria Inn, 189

I
IBM, 128, **129**, **130**, 133
Imperial Valley, 98, 153
Indian Wars, 182
Indians, 13, 15, 16, 26, 32, 39, 40, 53, 134, 159, 169, 188
Interstate 5: 17, 66, 68
Inyo County, 73, 74
Ives, Butler, 87

J
James, Jesse, **189**
Japanese, 162, 164, 184, 196
Johnson, Hiram, 73
Joint Board on Interstate Highways, 59
Jolan Road, 76, 115

K
Kansas City, 54
Kern County, 175
King City, 17, 38, 117, 164, 182, 201
King's Highway, 13, 16, 25, 43, 44, 47
Kite Expo, 202

L
La Brea Tar Pits, **169**
La Conchita, 153
La Mesa, 147
La Paz, 43
Lake Tahoe, 74
Landmarks Club, 17, 38, 47
Lankershim, James, 110
Legislative Routes, 55

Lincoln, Abraham, 87
Lompoc, 27, 30, 35, 94, **120**, 121, 123, **164**, 165, 181, 182, 198
Los Alamos, **194**, **195**, 201
Los Angeles: 13, 16, 17, 21, 26, 38, 39, 43, 51, 54, **55**, 57, 59, 60, 63, 66, **67**, 68, 74, 85, **91**, 92, 100, 108-110, 122, 135, 147, 153, 169, 177, 178, 181, 187, 188, 191, 201, 202
    Central Station, 100, 101
Los Angeles Chamber of Commerce, 47, 48
Los Angeles In Seven Days, 149
Los Angeles River, 39
Los Angeles Tripbook, 149
Los Angeles Union Passenger Terminal, **98**, 100, **102-104**, **107**, **108**, 202
Los Olivos, 123
Lummis, Charles Fletcher, 17, 38, 45, 60

M
Malibu, 17, 196, **197**
Malibu Potteries, 196
Marks-Fram Company, 110
Marshallia Dude Ranch, 182
McDonald, Angus, 13
Merchant Ships, 181, 184
Mexico, 13, 15, 32, 35, 37, 39, 44, 45, 53, 144, 150, 159, 164, 177, 182, 192, 202
Military: **65**, **176**, **177-185**
    Army, 139, 181-183, 184
    "Arsenal of Democracy", 179, 181, 185,
    Camp Merriam, 139, 183,
    Camp Roberts, 113, 182, 183, 189,
    Camp San Luis Obispo, 139, **140**, 183, **184**
    Campo de Cahuenga, 177
    Fort MacArthur, 184
    Korean War, 182, 184, 185
    Moffett Field, **180**, **181**
    Navy, 188, 198
    Point Mugu, 181
    Port Hueneme, 166, 181, **182**
    Vandenberg Air Force, 173, 183
Missions:
    California Missions, 15
    Dolores, 27, 33
    Hearst Mission Restoration Fund, 38
    La Purísima, 27, 30, 34, 35, 38, 60, 121, 123, 159, 198
    Ladder of Missions, 13, **14**, 25, 26, 39, 65, 130, 134, 143, 144, 147, 151, 165
    San Antonio de Padua, 30, 35, 38, **115**, 176, 182
    San Buenaventura, 27, **29**, **82**, 165
    San Carlos Borroméo, 25, **31**, 35, **73**
    San Diego, 13, **24**, 25, **28**, 39
    San Fernando, **29**, **35**, 39, **46**, **47**, 110, 149, 153, 159

San Gabriel, 27, **28**, 35, 38, **83**, 159
San José, **33**, 39, 159
San Juan Bautista, **31**, **38**
San Juan Capistrano, **28**, 34, **35**, 38, 159
San Luis Obispo, **30**, 48, **137**, **183**
San Luis Rey, 27, **28**
San Miguel, **2**, 30, **32**, 39, **115**, **118**, 119, 159, 188
San Rafael, **33**
Santa Barbara, 17, 27, **29**, 34, 35, **36**, **37**, 38, **45**, **142**, **143**, 147
    Queen of the Missions, 143
Santa Clara, **31**, 34, 39, 125
Santa Cruz, **32**, 39
Santa Ynéz, 13, **30**, 48, **49**, 58, 121, 123, 159
Solano, **33**, 43
Soledad, 27, **30**, 35, 39
Mission Memories, 44
Mission Memories: The Franciscan Missions…, 51
Mission Play, **8**, **41**, **44**, 149
Mission Trails Guide, **117**, 150, 151
Mojave Desert, 74
Montalvo Cutoff, **97**, 98
Monterey, 13, 16, 25, 26, 41, **57**, 125, 139, 143, **149**, 160, 181, 188, **189**, 195
Monterey Bay, **139**
Monterey County, 113, 153, 162, 175, 185
Morgan, Julia, 182
Morro Bay, 137, **138**, 184, 195
Movie Theaters, **193**

N
Native Daughters of the Golden West, 38, 47, 60
Neve, Governor Felipe de, 143
New England, 137
New Haven, 128
New Orleans, 92, 94
New York, 87, 122, 198

O
Oakland, 108
Oil: 17, 150, **168**, 169, **170-174**, 175, 178, 181
    Orcutt Oil Fields, 194
    Santa Maria Valley, 173
    Shell, 175, Texaco, 175
    Union Oil Station, 175
Oxnard, **97**, 98, 108, **166**, **167**, 181

P
Pacific Grove, 188
Pacific Ocean, **15**, **17**, 70, 119, 195, 201
Paderewski, Ignacy Jan, 189
Panama Canal, 73, 196

Panama-Pacific International Exposition, 21, 74, 196, **198**
Pasadena, 51, 147
Paso Robles, **68**, **97**, 135, 139, 188, **189**, 201
Pennsylvania, 94, 169
Photographers: 196
   McCurry Foto Company, 74
   Vroman, A.C., **51**, 147
Pico, Pio, 177
Pismo Beach, **77**, **78**, 169, **179**, 194, **195**, **196**, 202
Pitcher, Anna, 45, 47, 48, 60
Point Arguello, 184
Point Conception, 144
Point Fermin, 184
Port of Long Beach, 166
Port San Luis, **173**, 175, 184
Portola, Gaspar de, 13, 25, **26**, 134, 169
Post Cards: **18-21**, **110**, **111**, **155-157**
   Los Angeles Special, **110**, **111**
   Mitchell, Edward H., 21
   Teich, Curt, 19
Promontory, Utah, 87, **89**

R
Railroads:
   Amtrak-*Coast Starlight*, 17, **118**, 198, **200**, 201
   Atchison, Topeka & Santa Fe Railway, **54**, 92, 93
   Atlantic & Pacific Railroad, 87, **90**, 92
   Big Four: 87, 130
      Crocker, Charles 87, **88**, 187, 188
      Hopkins, Mark, 87, **88**
      Huntington, Collis P., 87, **88**, 92, 93
      Stanford, Leland, 87, **88**, 130, 170
   Central Pacific Railroad, 87
   Coast Line, 92, 94, 98, 164
   Daylight, **3**, **4**, 13, **16**, 17, **84**, 85, **98-100**, **102-109**, 201, **202**
      Route of the Missions, **98**
   San Joaquin *Daylight*, 108
   Lima Locomotive Works of Ohio, 100
   Pacific Coast Railway, 194
   San Francisco and San Jose Railroad, 85
   Southern Pacific: **12**, 13, **16**, 17, 40, 54, 85, 87, 92, 93, 94, **97**, 100, 106, 113, 115, 130, 147, 149, 164, 178, 187, 194, 201, Lark, 109, Railroad Depots: Central Station, **101**, San Jose, 87, San Luis Obispo, **95**, San Miguel, **116**, Ventura, **165**
   Union Pacific, 87, 93
   Union Pacific motion picture, **89**
Ramona, 15, **39**, **40**, 41, 43, 45
Redwood City, 66, 185
Refugio, 119
Restaurants:

Joe's Cafe, **192**
Lefty O'Doul's, **192**
Musso and Frank's, **191**
Original Joe's, **192**
The Hitching Post, **192**
Thelma Todd's Roadhouse, **196**
Wing's, **192**
Rincon, 54, **58**, **70**, **80**, **81**, 150
Roosevelt, Theodore, 15
Russia, 26

S
Sacramento, 74, 87, 153
Salinas: 16, 17, 57, 58, 92, 106, 117, 153, 162, **163**, 164, 166, 175, **193**, 194, 201, 202
   East of Eden, 162
   Rodeo, 202
Salinas River, 115, 117, 162, 163, 166
San Ardo, **174**, **175**, 185
San Diego, 13, 16, 17, 25, 26, 27, 43, 51, 55, 57, 59, 63, 66, 74, 143, 178, 181, 201
San Diego Panama-Pacific International Exposition, 73
San Fernando Valley, 57, 66, 92, 98, 153, 177
San Francisco, 13, 16, 17, 21, 25, **26**, 27, 33, 39, 43, 51, 54, 55, 57, 59, 63, 66, 68, 73, 74, 85, 87, 94, 100, 106, 108, 109, 125, 135, 144, 159, 170, 177, 178, 183, **187**, 188, 193, 196, 198, 201, 202
San Francisco Bay, 15, **26**, **27**, **125**, 181
San Joaquin, **53**, 85, 108, 153
San Jose: 16, 17, 26, 57, 66, 85, **87**, 94, 106, 125, **126-130**, **132**, 133, 141, 159, 160, 193, 202
   IBM, 128, **129**, **130**, **133**
   State University, 130, **131**, 202
San Luis Obispo, **50**, 70, **74**, **75**, 77, 92, 93, 94, 106, 108, 125, 134, 135, **136**, **137**, 139, **141**, 184, 189, **190**, 195, 201, 202
San Luis Obispo County, 139, **152**, **154**, 165, 169, 175, 194
San Marcos Pass, **52**, 71, 177
San Miguel, 113, 115, **117**, **118**, 163
San Pedro, 57, 178, 184
San Simeon, 137, **138**, 195
Santa Barbara, 16, 17, 26, 27, 51, 57, 68, 70, 92, 98, 108, 123, 143, 144, **145**, **147-151**, 173, 177, 184, 191, **193**, 194, 201, 202
Santa Barbara Channel, 173
Santa Barbara County: 17, 113, 119, 123, **144**, 165, 169, 170, 185, 189, 191, 193, 194, 202
   County Vintners Festival, 201
Santa Clara, 57, 125, 130, **131**, 159, 160, 166
Santa Cruz, **26**
Santa Lucia, 92, 94, 163

Santa Margarita, 92, **93**, 94
Santa Maria, 58, **72**, **172**, 173, 175, 182, 189
Santa Ynéz, **58**, **119**, 123, 149
Sierras, 74, 87
Silicon Valley, 128, **131**, 133, 159
Soledad, 92
Solvang, 58, 119, **120**, 121, 123
Sonoma, 26, 33, 43, 201
Spain, 13, 32, 143, 150
Spanish, 13, 15, 16, 25, 26, 34, 38, 39, 41, 43, 44, 60, 73, 125, 144, 147, 149, 150, 159, 169, 177, 187, 194, 201, 202
Spreckels, 166
Stagecoach, **52**, 144
Stanford University, 130, **131**, 202
Stearns Wharf, 144, 147
Stenner Creek trestle, **94**, **95**
Sterling, Christine, 60
Stockton, 85, 177
Studebaker Corporation
   EMF (Everitt-Metzger-Flanders), **50**, 74, **72-83**
Summerland, 150, 170, **172**
Sunnyvale, 181

T
Tehachapi, 85, **86**, 94, 108
Tingle, Minnie M., 1

U
Union, 153, 175
United States, 17, 19, 21, 39, 44, 58, 59, 139, 148, 160, 164, 166, 169, 170, 177, 184, 185, 187

V
Ventura, 17, 40, 54, **56**, 70, **80**, 92, 149, 153, 165, 166, 170, 181, **182**, 194, 201, 202

W
Winchester House of Mystery, 125, **128**
World War I, 110, 162, 178, 182, 183
World War II: 17, 19, 61, 65, 110, 121, 125, 128, 137, 139, 175, 178, 181, 184, 185, 189, 196
   Battle of Los Angeles, 184
   Ellwood Oil Field, 184
   Japanese, 184
   Richfield, 184
"World's Safest Beach", 193, **194**, 202
WPA Guide Book, 119, 143, 150

Illustration Credits

All post cards: Roger L. Titus Collection

pgs. 1, 4, 24, 49 right, 68 top left, 68 top right, 71 lower right, 120 top, 131 top left, lower right, 141 lower right, 151 right, 152, 164, 167, 174, 191 lower right, 192 top left, lower left, lower right, 194, 203: Josef K. Lesser

pgs. 2, 113, 114 top right, 114 lower, 115, 118 top left & right, 175, 184 right, 193 right: Roger L. Titus

pgs. 3, 84: Paul Jansson

pgs. 6, 7 – Contents: Chap. 1, 4 & 7 – Josef K. Lesser: Chap. 2 – Museum of Ventura County: Chap. 3 – Donald Duke, LARHF, Huntington Library: Chap. 5 & 6 – Tom Zimmerman Photography: Chap. 8 – Post Card: Roger L. Titus: Chap. 9 – Paul C. Koehler: Chap. 10 – Roger L. Titus

pgs. 8, 64: Huntington Library

pgs. 12, 54, 55, 66 top, 86, 90, 91, 98 right, 100, 102-103, 105, 144 right, 153, 158 lower left, 166 left, 171: LARHF Archive

pgs. 22, 23: Ronald Gustafson Collection

pgs. 27 top right, 32 lower right, 158 left: Roger L. Titus Collection

pgs. 34, 41 left, 42, 43, 45 left, 47, 59 lower right, 60, 62 right, 110, 111, 117 left, 142, 145 left, 168, 180, 181 lower, 186, 199: Tom Zimmerman Archives

pgs. 38, 60, 62 left, 68 lower, 85, 114 top left, 117 right, 118 lower, 138 top right, 192 top right: Tom Zimmerman Photography

pgs. 39, 40: Ramona Bowl Amphitheatre

pgs. 46, 63: Los Angeles Public Library

pgs. 48 left, 120 lower, 132, 169, 193 left, 195 right: Jo Ann Lesser

pgs. 48 center, 58 lower right, 59 top, 59 lower left, 69, 93, 94-95, 95 lower right, 97 lower, 116, 134, 135, 136 top, 137 top, 137 lower, 140, 144 left, 154, 159, 179 lower right, 183, 184 left, 190 top left, 195 top left, 196: History Center of San Luis Obispo County

pgs. 50, 67, 69, 72-83: California Department of Transportation

p. 51: Seaver Center for Western History Research, Los Angeles County Natural History Museum

pgs. 52, 58 top right, 71 top left and right, 112, 119, 121, 122, 123: Buellton Historical Society

pgs. 53, 57, 58 top left, 197: Automobile Club of Southern California

pgs. 56, 70 top left, 70 lower right, 165: Museum of Ventura County

p. 61: Pasadena Museum of History

pgs. 87, 124, 126, 127, 129, 130, 133, 161.163 left: Sourisseau Academy for State & Local History, San Jose State University

p. 88: E. B. Crocker Collection, Crocker Art Museum

pgs. 89, 101, 147: Bison Archives, Marc Wanamaker

pgs. 96, 200: Mark Borja

p. 97 top left: Bruce Petty Collection

p. 98 left: Mike Jarel Archive

pgs. 99, 106, 107, 108, 109 top & lower: Donald Duke, LARHF, Huntington Library

p. 104: Ralph Melching

p. 137 lower: Leif Casagrande, Apple Farm Inn

p. 160 top left and right: Lora Schraft

p. 160 lower left & right: Gilroy Historical Society Collection

p. 176: National Park Service, Fort Hunter Liggett Special Resources Study

pgs. 179 top, 185: Paul C. Koehler

pgs. 179 lower left, 181 top right: JKL Archive

p. 182: Naval Base Ventura County (NBVC) Port Hueneme/Point Mugu; and Vandenberg Air Force Base, 30th Space Wing, Community Relations

p. 189 lower: The Ellison Collection

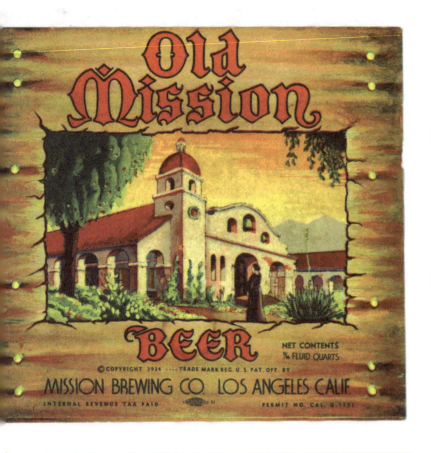